BEN JONSON

The Alchemist

EDITED BY

Gerald Eades Bentley

PRINCETON UNIVERSITY

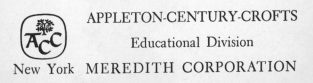

APPLETON-CENTURY-CROFTS

Educational Division

New York MEREDITH CORPORATION

Introduction

When *The Alchemist* was first performed by Shakespeare's company, the King's Men, at the Blackfriars theatre in London in the autumn or winter of 1610, Jonson was already widely known as one of the leading English men of letters. He had written or collaborated in a dozen or more plays; he had been recognized as the best writer of court masques, those spectacular entertainments at the court of King James about which all London talked; he was widely admired as the most learned poet and critic of the time.

Jonson's reputation was due in part to the fact that he was the most articulate dramatic critic of his day. He pointed again and again to the shortcomings of contemporary plays, as he saw them; he stated repeatedly what he thought plays ought to be; and he had the temerity to announce that his plays were "such as other plays should be." He thought that comedies should not be like Shakespeare's *As You Like It* and *Twelfth Night* or Robert Greene's *Scottish History of James IV* and *Friar Bacon and Friar Bungay*. Such plays, set in the Forest of Arden or Illyria or thirteenth century Oxford, were too far removed from everyday London life. Jonson thought that comedy should contribute to the improvement of society and therefore should depict contemporary Londoners as they really lived in his day. He objected therefore to the unnatural mixture of classes which characterized romantic comedies—a countess in love with a page, as in *Twelfth Night*, a king's son in love with a game keeper's daughter, as in *Friar Bacon and Friar Bungay,* or two princesses wandering about in a forest with a clown, as in *As You Like It*.

Jonson also objected to the romantic plots and the highly idealized language of many Elizabethan plays. Characters in comedies, he thought, should undergo experiences common in London, and they should speak, not like Viola and Orsino in *Twelfth Night,* but like the people one met on the streets and in the shops of the town. As he phrased it, comedy should deal with "deeds and language such as men do use." The purpose of comedy should not be mere entertainment, but a picture of contemporary follies so presented that, by laughing at its own vices seen on the stage, the audience might be led to more rational conduct.

Elizabethan plays in general were too sprawling in their structure and too romantic in their characterization to suit Jonson. He agreed with the classic critics that the action of a play should be confined to one city and if possible to a period of less than twenty-four hours. Characters should consistently display their dominant characteristics or humours: the jealous man should exhibit his jealousy on all occasions, the greedy man his greed, the gullible man his credulity, the vain man his vanity. No human being, of course, ever succeeds in living up to his own principles at all times, and Jonson, like others, sometimes produced plays which did not measure up to his own standards. His best comedies, however, are remarkable applications of the principles which he advocated. None of them more fully exemplifies the type of comedy which Jonson thought London should have than *The Alchemist*.

This play is not only set in contemporary London, but Jonson has carefully indicated the precise district in London—the very one in which the theatre in which it was first given is located. The time is not the distant past nor even the approximate present; it is the very year of the first performance. Jonson repeatedly indicates that the action takes place during a London epidemic of the plague. This fatal and terrifying disease was one of the great horrors of Jacobean London. When the epidemic was raging, thousands died, often on the streets, and the terrified citizens lived in dread, or, if they were well-to-do like Lovewit in the play, fled the town and left their houses in the hands of servants like Jeremy, *alias* Face, *alias* Lungs. Such epidemics of the plague occurred in 1609 and 1610, and probably a number of well-to-do people in the Blackfriars audience at the first performance of *The Alchemist* had, like Lovewit, recently returned to their London houses after the plague of 1610.

The Alchemist further exemplifies Jonson's standards of play-writing in its avoidance of the unusual mixture of classes which characterizes romantic comedies like *Mucedorus, George-a-Greene,* or *As You Like It.* In the *dramatis personae* of *The Alchemist* there are, on the one hand, no kings or queens, princes or nobles, and on the other no beggars or dairy maids. The characters are representative of the upper and lower middle classes commonly found in social or business contact in Jacobean London—a tobacconist, a gambler, a butler, a foolish young country gentleman and his sister, a prostitute, a confidence man, a Puritan minister. In the play these ordinary London characters undergo experiences which might take place in the English capital any day. They are the vicitms or the perpetrators of swindles like those reported daily in modern metropolitan police courts. Of course the crooks use specific Jacobean tricks and not the tricks of twentieth century confidence men, but the characters, the motives, and the general methods of swindlers and swindled are much the same in the seventeenth century and the twentieth.

The particular type of swindle which Jonson has Face and Subtle use most extensively on their victims is that of the fake alchemist. Today we are familiar with swindles like palmistry, astrology, numerology, the badger game, marked cards, loaded dice, bogus companies, rubber checks, "protection," fraudulent advertising, spiritualism—several of which Face, Subtle, and Doll use—but the fake alchemist rarely appears in modern police court news. His was a favorite device of London crooks in Jonson's time because most people then were confused and uncertain about the possibilities of chemistry and physics. For centuries the natural scientists had believed in the essential unity of all matter, and that matter might be transmuted from one state to another. The transmutation of baser metals to gold was only one of many possibilities, but it was the one most appealing to avaricious men. Hundreds of alchemists, many of them men of great learning and no little laboratory experience, had worked in Europe in the middle ages and the Renaissance. They had tried many experiments, but most often they had attempted to develop the philosopher's stone (sometimes called the magisterium or the elixir or the quintessence), the perfect universal essence of all matter which because of its perfection and universality might do all things for all men. These experiments of the alchemists were widely but ignorantly discussed. What a chance for clever crooks! Many of them seized the opportunity and practised vigorously. A few of the cleverest, like John Dee and Edward Kelley, whom Jonson mentions in his play, had practised on kings and queens and great nobles. The pretensions of Subtle in *The Alchemist* are no greater than those of Edward Kelley; Jonson simply makes Subtle's true character clearer to the audience than Kelley's character was to his victims. This is a familiar difference between swindling in plays and swindling in real life.

Jonson's Subtle is by no means an ignorant crook. He shows a wide and accurate knowledge of the many books on alchemy; he is familiar with all the current scientific terms and methods; he presents a scientific argument for the theory of alchemy which even the sceptical Surly cannot answer. Subtle is certainly a crook and not a scientist, but like many crooks he has studied long and painstakingly in his profession. Probably none of the members of Jonson's audience understood all the learned terms that Subtle used, but they knew a few, and, having heard many of the others in a scientific context, they took their scientific accuracy on faith, just as most modern patients do when listening to the doctor.

Jonson has thus selected for his play characters from everyday London life, and he shows them engaged in swindles which were common enough in London in 1610. Their deeds are "such as men do use," and their language is too. This further fidelity of Jonson to his realistic principles causes one of the chief difficulties of the play for modern readers. People like those depicted in *The Alchemist* are not noted for the purity of their speech. They resort constantly to slang, vulgarisms, and colloquialisms, types of language which soon pass out of fashion. Today some of this accurately transcribed speech of the Londoners of 300 years ago is as difficult to understand as "Jeez, that hep cat sure can send me!" will be 300 years from now. Many of the expressions must be explained in footnotes, and some of them are unintelligible even to the scholars who write the footnotes.

The characters of *The Alchemist* are not only familiar types of Londoners of the year 1610, but they are set forth in such a way that the audience may be edified as well as amused by their conduct. Jonson had said that comedies ought to "show an image of the times and sport with human follies." The follies of the gullible Dapper, the greedy, sensual Mammon, the childish Drugger, and the silly, bumptious Kastril are made plain enough and ridiculous enough in the play for any spectator to understand and to profit by if he himself had any such tendencies. The Puritan minister, Tribulation Wholesome, and the deacon of his congregation, Ananias, are of a different order. These religious hypocrites are portrayed by Jonson as more vicious than the other gulls. In Act II, Scene

5, they are ready to cheat orphans if their parents had not been Puritans; they preach nonsense about the imaginary sins of other people; in II, 2, and IV, 7, they are willing to engage in counterfeiting for the profit of the congregation. To Jonson these Puritans seemed more contemptible and less amusing than the other gulls of Face and Subtle. His portrayal of the sect, and even of some of the congregations, which furnished the passenger list for the ship Mayflower in 1620 may well be contrasted with some of the New England Puritans' writings about themselves.

With all his care in *The Alchemist* to adhere to the principles he thinks fitting for comedy, Jonson never allows the play to become pedantic. Though the play is plotted with such exquisite skill that Coleridge once said it had one of the three best plots in all literature, it is boisterous and rollicking from beginning to end. When the comedy is performed, the audience is always struck by the rapid pace of the action and the masculine virility of the scenes. In his life Jonson was a hearty and violent man; much of his own gusto appears in *The Alchemist*.

The Principal Dates in Jonson's Life

1572   Jonson was born, probably in London.

c. 1583-c. 1589   He was a student at Westminster School, London.

c. 1589   He was apprentice bricklayer to his step-father.

c. 1594   Served as a soldier against the Spaniards in Flanders.

1598, September 22   Killed the actor, Gabriel Spencer, in a duel.

1598, September   *Every Man in His Humour* performed by the Lord Chamberlain's company with William Shakespeare in the cast.

1601   Jonson's satiric comedy *Poetaster* attacking his enemies, John Marston and Thomas Dekker and others, performed by the Children of the Chapel at Blackfriars theatre.

1601   Thomas Dekker's play *Satiromastix*, ridiculing Jonson, acted by the Lord Chamberlain's company at the Globe a few weeks after *Poetaster*. These two plays are the principal dramatic documents in the "War of the Theatres."

1603, March 25   James I, a learned man and an admirer of Jonson's work, proclaimed King of England.

1603   *Sejanus*, Jonson's learned tragedy of Roman history, performed by the King's Men at the Globe theatre with William Shakespeare in the cast.

c. 1603   The famous society of Jonson's admirers and friends called "The Tribe of Ben" began meeting at the Mermaid Tavern.

1605, January 6   *The Masque of Blackness*, the first of Jonson's spectacular entertainments, presented before the King and court at Whitehall palace with Queen Anne as one of the performers.

1605   Jonson, Chapman, and Marston jailed for satire of the Scots and of King James himself in their play *Eastward Ho*.

1606   *Volpone or the Fox* acted by the King's Men at the Globe theatre.

1608, February 9   *Lord Haddington's Masque*, sometimes called *The Hue and Cry after Cupid*, written for the wedding of Viscount Haddington and Lady Elizabeth Radcliffe, presented before the King and court.

1609   *Epicoene or the Silent Woman* acted by the Children of the Queen's Revels.

1610, Autumn   *The Alchemist* acted by the King's Men at the Blackfriars theatre.

1611   *Catiline*, the second of Jonson's learned tragedies of Roman history, acted by the King's Men.

1612, January 6   *Love Restored*, a masque, presented at Whitehall palace before the King and court.

1612-1613   In France as tutor to the son of Sir Walter Raleigh.

1614, October 31   *Bartholomew Fair* acted at the Hope theatre on the Bankside by the Lady Elizabeth's Men.

1616, February   King James granted a pension to Jonson.

1616   A collection of Jonson's plays, masques, and poems published under the title *The Works of Benjamin Jonson.*

1618, Summer and Autumn   Jonson went on a walking tour to Edinburgh, where he was made an honorary burgess of the city. For two or three weeks he was the guest of William Drummond, of Hawthornden, who kept notes of his conversations.

1619, July   Jonson formally inducted as honorary Master of Arts by Oxford University.

1621, August 3 and 5 and September   *The Gypsies Metamorphosed,* Jonson's humorous masque, presented at the country houses of the Marquis of Buckingham and the Earl of Rutland and at Windsor Castle.

1625   Death of Jonson's admirer, King James I, and accession of Charles I.

1626   *The Staple of News* performed by the King's Men.

1628   Made City Chronologer for London.

1632   Jonson's last comedy, *The Magnetic Lady,* performed by the King's Men at Blackfriars.

1637   Died August 6; buried August 9 in Westminster Abbey.

1638   *Jonsonus Virbius,* a collection of poems in praise of Jonson by thirty-one of the leading literary men of the time, published.

To the Reader

If thou beest more, thou art an understander, and then I trust thee. If thou art one that tak'st up, and but a pretender, beware at what hands thou receiv'st thy commodity; for thou wert never more fair in the way to be coz'ned than in this age in poetry, especially in plays: wherein now the concupiscence of jigs and dances so reigneth, as to run away from nature and be afraid of her is the only point of art that tickles the spectators. But how out of purpose and place do I name art, when the professors are grown so obstinate contemners of it, and presumers on their own naturals, as they are deriders of all diligence that way, and, by simple mocking at the terms when they understand not the things, think to get off wittily with their ignorance! Nay, they are esteem'd the more learned and sufficient for this by the multitude, through their excellent vice of judgment. For they commend writers as they do fencers or wrastlers; who, if they come in robustiously and put for it with a great deal of violence, are receiv'd for the braver fellows; when many times their own rudeness is the cause of their disgrace, and a little touch of their adversary gives all that boisterous force the foil. I deny not but that these men who always seek to do more than enough may some time happen on some thing that is good and great—but very seldom, and when it comes, it doth not recompense the rest of their ill. It sticks out, perhaps, and is more eminent, because all is sordid and vile about it; as lights are more discern'd in a thick darkness than a faint shadow. I speak not this out of a hope to do good on any man against his will; for I know, if it were put to the question of theirs and mine, the worse would find more suffrages, because the most favour common errors. But I give thee this warning, that there is a great difference between those that (to gain the opinion of copy) utter all they can, however unfitly, and those that use election and a mean. For it is only the disease of the unskillful to think rude things greater than polish'd, or scatter'd more numerous than compos'd.

THE PERSONS OF THE PLAY

SUBTLE [a rogue who poses as an alchemist]

FACE [really Jeremy, butler to Lovewit, who has grown a beard and disguises himself, sometimes as an army captain and sometimes as Lungs, laboratory assistant to the alchemist, Subtle]

DOL COMMON [a prostitute who acts as accomplice to Face and Subtle]

DAPPER [a gullible lawyer's clerk]

ABEL DRUGGER [proprietor of a small tobacco shop]

LOVEWIT [a prosperous London gentleman, Jeremy's (*alias* Face's) master, and owner of the house in Blackfriars where all the action takes place]

SIR EPICURE MAMMON [a swaggering, avaricious knight]

PERTINAX SURLY [a gambler, friend of Mammon]

TRIBULATION WHOLESOME [Pastor of a congregation of fanatical English Puritans who have emigrated to Amsterdam]

ANANIAS [Deacon of the congregation; a violently fanatical Puritan, formerly a tailor]

KASTRIL [a gullible, well-to-do youth, come up to London from the country to learn how to be a city brawler]

DAME PLIANT [his sister, an attractive but stupid young widow of 19]

Neighbors, Officers of the Law, a Parson

THE SCENE

[Lovewit's house in the Blackfriars district of London.
Autumn, 1610.]

THE ARGUMENT

T he sickness hot, a master quit, for fear,
H is house in town, and left one servant there.
E ase him corrupted, and gave means to know
A Cheater and his punk, who now brought low,
L eaving their narrow practice, were become
C oz'ners at large; and only wanting some
H ouse to set up, with him they here contract,
E ach for a share, and all begin to act.
M uch company they draw, and much abuse,
 I n casting figures, telling fortunes, news,   10
 S elling of flies, flat bawdry, with the stone;
T ill it, and they, and all in fume are gone.

PROLOGUE

FORTUNE, that favours fools, these two short hours
   We wish away, both for your sakes and ours,
Judging spectators; and desire in place,
   To th' author justice, to ourselves but grace.
Our scene is London, 'cause we would make known,
   No country's mirth is better than our own.
No clime breeds better matter for your whore,
   Bawd, squire, imposter, many persons more,
Whose manners, now call'd humours, feed the stage;
   And which have still been subject for the rage   10
Or spleen of comic writers. Though this pen
   Did never aim to grieve, but better men,
Howe'er the age he lives in doth endure
   The vices that she breeds, above their cure.
But when the wholesome remedies are sweet,
   And, in their working gain and profit meet,
He hopes to find no spirit so much diseas'd,
   But will with such fair correctives be pleas'd.
For here he doth not fear who can apply.
   If there be any that will sit so nigh   20
Unto the stream, to look what it doth run,
   They shall find things, they'd think, or wish, were done;
They are so natural follies, but so shown,
   As even the doers may see, and yet not own.

1 **hot** raging 4 **punk** mistress, whore 6 **Coz'ners** swindlers 10 **casting figures** calculating horoscopes 11 **flies** familiar spirits **stone** philosopher's stone 12 **fume** smoke 8 **squire** pander 10 **still** always

THE ALCHEMIST
by Ben Jonson

Act I

Scene I

[*Enter* FACE, *wearing a captain's uniform, and* SUBTLE, *carrying a vial of chemical. They are quarrelling violently.* DOL COMMON *follows them in.*]

FACE   Believe 't, I will.

SUBTLE   Thy worst. I fart at thee.

DOL COMMON   Ha' you your wits? Why, gentlemen! for love—

FACE   Sirrah, I'll strip you—

SUBTLE   What to do? Lick figs
Out at my—

FACE   Rogue, rogue!—out of all your sleights.

DOL COMMON   Nay, look ye, sovereign, general, are you madmen?

SUBTLE   O, let the wild sheep loose. I'll gum your silks
With good strong water, an you come.

DOL COMMON   Will you have
10 The neighbours hear you? Will you betray all?
Hark! I hear somebody.

FACE   Sirrah—

SUBTLE   I shall mar
All that the tailor has made, if you approach.

FACE   You most notorious whelp, you insolent slave,
Dare you do this?

SUBTLE   Yes, faith; yes, faith.

FACE   Why, who
Am I, my mongrel, who am I?

SUBTLE   I'll tell you,
Since you know not yourself.

FACE   Speak lower, rogue.

4 **Lick figs** (*see* Rabelais, Bk. IV, Ch. 45) 5 **sleights** tricks

2

SUBTLE   Yes. You were once (time's not long past) the good,

Honest, plain, livery-three-pound-thrum, that kept

Your master's worship's house here in the Friars, 20

For the vacations—

FACE   Will you be so loud?

SUBTLE   Since, by my means, translated suburb-captain.

FACE   By your means, doctor dog!

SUBTLE   Within man's memory,

All this I speak of.

FACE   Why, I pray you, have I

Been countenanc'd by you, or you by me?

Do but 'collect, sir, where I met you first.

SUBTLE   I do not hear well.

FACE   Not of this, I think it.

But I shall put you in mind, sir;—at Pie-corner,

Taking your meal of steam in, from cooks' stalls,

Where, like the father of hunger, you did walk 30

Piteously costive, with your pinch'd-horn-nose,

And your complexion of the Roman wash,

Stuck full of black and melancholic worms,

Like powder-corns shot at th' artillery-yard.

SUBTLE   I wish you could advance your voice a little.

FACE   When you went pinn'd up in the several rags

Y' had rak'd and pick'd from dunghills, before day;

Your feet in mouldy slippers, for your kibes;

A felt of rug, and a thin threaden cloak,

That scarce would cover your no-buttocks—

SUBTLE   So, sir! 40

FACE   When all your alchemy, and your algebra,

Your minerals, vegetals, and animals,

Your conjuring, coz'ning, and your dozen of trades,

Could not relieve your corpse with so much linen

Would make you tinder, but to see a fire;

I ga' you count'nance, credit for your coals,

Your stills, your glasses, your materials;

Built you a furnace, drew you customers,

Advanc'd all your black arts; lent you, beside,

A house to practise in—

19 **livery . . . thrum** under paid drudge 20 **Friars** Blackfriars, a fashionable section of London 22 **suburb** suburbs were low districts 25 **countenanc'd** sanctioned 34 **powder-corns** grains of powder 38 **kibes** chilblains 39 **felt of rug** hat of coarse material

50   SUBTLE   Your master's house!
      FACE   Where you have studied the more thriving skill
Of bawdry since.
      SUBTLE   Yes, in your master's house.
You and the rats here kept possession.
Make it not strange. I know you were one could keep
The buttery-hatch still lock'd, and save the chippings,
Sell the dole beer to aqua vitae men,
The which, together with your Christmas vails
At post-and-pair, your letting out of counters,
Made you a pretty stock, some twenty marks,
60 And gave you credit to converse with cobwebs
Here, since your mistress' death hath broke up house.
      FACE   You might talk softlier, rascal.
      SUBTLE   No, you scarab,
I'll thunder you in pieces. I will teach you
How to beware to tempt a Fury again
That carries tempest in his hand and voice.
      FACE   The place has made you valiant.
      SUBTLE   No, your clothes.
Thou vermin, have I ta'en thee out of dung,
So poor, so wretched, when no living thing
Would keep thee company, but a spider or worse?
70 Rais'd thee from brooms and dust and wat'ring-pots?
Sublim'd thee, and exalted thee, and fix'd thee
I' the third region, call'd our state of grace?
Wrought thee to spirit, to quintessence, with pains
Would twice have won me the philosopher's work?
Put thee in words and fashion? made thee fit
For more than ordinary fellowships?
Giv'n thee thy oaths, thy quarrelling dimensions?
Thy rules to cheat at horse-race, cock-pit, cards,
Dice, or whatever gallant tincture else?
80 Made thee a second in mine own great art?
And have I this for thanks! Do you rebel?
Do you fly out i' the projection?
Would you be gone now?

51 **skill** art, trade 54 **Make . . . strange** Do not pretend to forget
55 **chippings** . . **men** Doles of waste bread, or "chippings," and beer
were distributed to the poor from great houses. Subtle accuses Face of
selling the beer to liquor-dealers 57 **vails** tips 58 **post-and-pair** a card
game 62 **scarab** dung beetle 73 **Sublim'd . . . quintessence** technical
terms in alchemy 77 **quarrelling dimensions** rules for conducting a quarrel 79 **tincture** accomplishment 82 **i' the projection** when success is near

DOL COMMON   Gentlemen, what mean you?
Will you mar all?

    SUBTLE   Slave, thou hadst had no name—

    DOL COMMON   Will you undo yourselves with civil **war?**

    SUBTLE   Never been known, past *equi clibanum,*
The heat of horse-dung, under ground, in cellars,
Or an ale-house darker than deaf John's; been lost
To all mankind, but laundresses and tapsters,
Had not I been.

    DOL COMMON   Do you know who hears you, sovereign?   **90**

    FACE   Sirrah—

    DOL COMMON   Nay, general, I thought you were civil.

    FACE   I shall turn desperate, if you grow thus loud.

    SUBTLE   And hang thyself, I care not.

    FACE   Hang thee, **collier,**
And all thy pots and pans, in picture I will,
Since thou hast mov'd me—

    DOL COMMON   [*Aside.*] O, this 'll o'erthrow all.

    FACE   Write thee up bawd in Paul's; have all **thy tricks**
Of coz'ning with a hollow coal, dust, scrapings,
Searching for things lost, with a sieve and shears,
Erecting figures in your rows of houses,
And taking in of shadows with a glass,   **100**
Told in red letters; and a face cut for thee,
Worse than Gamaliel Ratsey's.

    DOL COMMON   Are you sound?
Ha' you your senses, masters?

    FACE   I will have
A book, but barely reckoning thy impostures,
Shall prove a true philosopher's stone to printers.

    SUBTLE   Away, you trencher-rascal!

    FACE   Out, you dog-leech!
The vomit of all prisons—

    DOL COMMON   Will you be
Your own destructions, gentlemen?

    FACE   Still spew'd out
For lying too heavy o' the basket.

    SUBTLE   Cheater!

86 **equi clibanum** translated in next line 96 **Paul's** St. Paul's Cathedral,
a place of resort for business and pleasure, where notices were often
posted 101 **thy tricks . . . for thee** familiar tricks of Elizabethan
swindlers 102 **Ratsey** a notorious highwayman, executed 1605, who
wore a hideous mask **sound** sane 109 **lying . . . basket** eating more than
his share of prison rations

FACE   Bawd!

SUBTLE   Cow-herd!

FACE   Conjurer!

SUBTLE   Cutpurse!

FACE   Witch!

110 DOL COMMON   O me!
We are ruin'd! lost! Ha' you no more regard
To your reputations? Where's your judgment? 'Slight,
Have yet some care of me, o' your republic—
    FACE   Away this brach! I'll bring thee, rogue, within
The statute of sorcery, tricesimo tertio
Of Harry the Eight: ay, and perhaps thy neck
Within a noose, for laund'ring gold and barbing it.
    DOL COMMON   You'll bring your head within a coxcomb,
will you?

She catcheth out FACE *his sword, and breaks* SUBTLE's *glass.*

120 And you, sir, with your menstrue!—Gather it up.
'Sdeath, you abominable pair of stinkards,
Leave off your barking, and grow one again,
Or, by the light that shines, I'll cut your throats.
I'll not be made a prey unto the marshal
For ne'er a snarling dog-bolt o' you both.
Ha' you together cozen'd all this while,
And all the world, and shall it now be said,
You've made most courteous shift to cozen yourselves?
[*To* FACE.] You will accuse him! You will "bring him in
130 Within the statute!" Who shall take your word?
A whoreson, upstart, apocryphal captain,
Whom not a Puritan in Blackfriars will trust
So much as for a feather! [*To* SUBTLE.] And you, too,
Will give the cause, forsooth? You will insult,
And claim a primacy in the divisions?
You must be chief? As if you only had
The powder to project with, and the work
Were not begun out of equality!

---

113 **republic** fraternity 114 **brach** bitch 115 **statute . . . Eight** the first
law against witchcraft, 33 Henry VIII (*i.e.,* 1541) 117 **laundring gold
and barbing it** washing gold in acid; chipping coins 118 **coxcomb**
fool's cap 120 **menstrue** a liquid which dissolves solids 125 **dog-bolt**
contemptible fellow 133 **feather** feathers and other costume accessories
were sold in the Blackfriars district, especially by Puritans 134 **insult**
boast 135 **primacy** first choice 137 **powder to project** the philosopher's
stone to transmute metals

The venter tripartite! All things in common!
Without priority! 'Sdeath! you perpetual curs,   140
Fall to your couples again, and cozen kindly,
And heartily, and lovingly, as you should,
And lose not the beginning of a term,
Or, by this hand, I shall grow factious too,
And take my part, and quit you.
    FACE   'T is his fault;
He ever murmurs, and objects his pains,
And says the weight of all lies upon him.
    SUBTLE Why, so it does.
    DOL COMMON   How does it? Do not we
Sustain our parts?
    SUBTLE   Yes, but they are not equal.
    DOL COMMON Why, if your part exceed to-day, I hope   150
Ours may to-morrow match it.
    SUBTLE   Ay, they may.
    DOL COMMON May, murmuring mastiff? Ay, and do.
Death on me! Help me to throttle him.
        [*Seizes* SUBTLE *by the throat.*]
    SUBTLE Dorothy! Mistress Dorothy!
'Ods precious, I'll do anything. What do you mean?
    DOL COMMON Because o' your fermentation and cibation?
    SUBTLE Not I, by heaven—
    DOL COMMON   Your Sol and Luna—[*To* FACE.] Help me.
    SUBTLE Would I were hang'd then! I'll conform myself.
    DOL COMMON Will you, sir? Do so then, and quickly: 160
swear.
    SUBTLE What should I swear?
    DOL COMMON   To leave your faction, sir,
And labour kindly in the common work.
    SUBTLE Let me not breathe if I meant aught beside.
I only used those speeches as a spur
To him.
    DOL COMMON I hope we need no spurs, sir. Do we?
    FACE 'Slid, prove to-day who shall shark best.
    SUBTLE Agreed.
    DOL COMMON Yes, and work close and friendly.

139 **venter tripartite** threefold agreement 143 **term** *i.e.*, one of the
terms of the law courts, when ignorant country people came to town and
the social season was at its height 156 **fermentation and cibation** processes in alchemy 158 **Sol and Luna** gold and silver 162 **faction** dissen-
sion

SUBTLE 'Slight, the knot
170 Shall grow the stronger for this breach, with me.

[*They shake hands.*]

DOL COMMON Why, so, my good baboons! Shall we go make
A sort of sober, scurvy, precise neighbors,
That scarce have smil'd twice sin' the king came in,
A feast of laughter at our follies? Rascals,
Would run themselves from breath, to see me ride,
Or you t' have but a hole to thrust your heads in,
For which you should pay ear-rent? No, agree.
And may Don Provost ride a-feasting long,
180 In his old velvet jerkin and stain'd scarfs,
My noble sovereign, and worthy general,
Ere we contribute a new crewel garter
To his most worsted worship.

SUBTLE Royal Dol!
Spoken like Claridiana, and thyself.

FACE For which at supper, thou shalt sit in triumph,
And not be styl'd Dol Common, but Dol Proper,
Dol Singular; the longest cut at night
Shall draw thee for his Dol Particular.

[*Bell rings without.*]

SUBTLE Who's that? One rings. To the window, Dol!—
190 Pray heav'n
The master do not trouble us this quarter.

FACE O, fear not him. While there dies one a week
O' the plague, he's safe from thinking toward London.
Beside, he's busy at his hop-yards now;
I had a letter from him. If he do,
He'll send such word, for airing o' the house,
As you shall have sufficient time to quit it.
Though we break up a fortnight, 't is no matter.

SUBTLE Who is it, Dol?

173 **sort** group **precise** puritanical 174 **sin' . . . in** since James I
ascended the throne in 1603, seven years before the play 176 **ride** *i.e.*,
on a cart, a punishment for whores 177 **hole . . . in** the pillory 178 **pay
ear-rent** have your ears cut off, a police court punishment 179 **Don
Provost** the hangman, who got the clothes of executed criminals
184 **Claridiana** the heroine of a popular romance, *The Mirror of Knight-
hood* 198 **Though . . . matter** Even though we stay here another fortnight, we will still be safe

DOL COMMON   A fine young quodling.

FACE   O,

My lawyer's clerk, I lighted on last night,   200
In Holborn, at the Dagger. He would have
(I told you of him) a familiar,
To rifle with at horses, and win cups.

DOL COMMON   O, let him in.

SUBTLE   Stay. Who shall do 't?

FACE   Get you
Your robes on; I will meet him, as going out.

DOL COMMON   And what shall I do?

FACE   Not be seen; away! [*Exit* DOL COMMON.]
Seem you very reserv'd.

SUBTLE   Enough. [*Exit.*]

FACE   [*In a loud voice as he goes to the door.*]
                    God be wi' you, sir.
I pray you, let him know that I was here:
His name is Dapper. I would gladly have stay'd, but—   210

Scene II

[DAPPER *within.*]   Captain, I am here.

FACE   Who's that?—He's come, I think, Doctor.
                    [FACE *admits* DAPPER.]
Good faith, sir, I was going away.

DAPPER   In truth,
I'm very sorry, Captain.

FACE   But I thought
Sure I should meet you.

DAPPER   Ay, I'm very glad.
I had a scurvy writ or two to make,
And I had lent my watch last night to one
That dines to-day at the shrieve's, and so was robbed
Of my pass-time.

        [*Re-enter* SUBTLE *in his velvet cap and gown.*]

                    Is this the cunning-man?

FACE   This is his worship.

199 quodling green apple, youth 201 Dagger a notorious tavern
202 familiar familiar spirit, "fly" 203 rifle gamble 8 shrieve's sheriff's
9 pass-time watch

DAPPER   Is he a doctor?

10   FACE   Yes.

DAPPER   And ha' you broke with him, Captain?

FACE   Ay.

DAPPER   And how?

FACE   Faith, he does make the matter, sir, so dainty,
I know not what to say.

DAPPER   Not so, good Captain.

FACE   Would I were fairly rid on 't, believe me.

DAPPER   Nay, now you grieve me, sir. Why should you
wish so?
I dare assure you, I'll not be ungrateful.

FACE   I cannot think you will, sir. But the law
20 Is such a thing—and then he says, Read's matter
Falling so lately—

DAPPER   Read! he was an ass,
And dealt, sir, with a fool.

FACE   It was a clerk, sir.

DAPPER   A clerk!

FACE   Nay, hear me, sir. You know the law
Better, I think—

DAPPER   I should, sir, and the danger:
You know, I show'd the statute to you.

FACE   You did so.

DAPPER   And will I tell then! By this hand of flesh,
Would it might never write good courthand more,
If I discover. What do you think of me,
That I am a chiaus?

FACE   What's that?

30   DAPPER   The Turk was here.
As one would say, do you think I am a Turk?

FACE   I'll tell the Doctor so.

DAPPER   Do, good sweet Captain.

FACE   Come, noble Doctor, pray thee, let's prevail;
This is the gentleman, and he is no chiaus.

SUBTLE   Captain, I have return'd you all my answer.
I would do much, sir, for your love—But this
I neither may, nor can.

FACE   Tut, do not say so.

---

11 **broke** broached the subject   13 **make . . . dainty** has such scruples
20 **Read** a magician indicted in 1608   22 **clerk** Read had dealt with
a law clerk (like Dapper) named Tobias Matthews   29 **discover**
reveal

You deal now with a noble fellow, Doctor,
One that will thank you richly; and he's no chiaus.
Let that, sir, move you.

SUBTLE   Pray you, forbear—

FACE   He has   40
Four angels here.

SUBTLE   You do me wrong, good sir.

FACE   Doctor, wherein? To tempt you with these spirits?

SUBTLE   To tempt my art and love, sir, to my peril.
'Fore heav'n, I scarce can think you are my friend,
That so would draw me to apparent danger.

FACE   I draw you! A horse draw you, and a halter,
You, and your flies together—

DAPPER   Nay, good Captain.

FACE   That know no difference of men.

SUBTLE   Good words, sir.

FACE   Good deeds, sir, Doctor Dogs'-meat. 'Slight, I bring
you   50
No cheating Clim o' the Cloughs or Claribels,
That look as big as five-and-fifty, and flush;
And spit out secrets like hot custard—

DAPPER   Captain!

FACE   Nor any melancholic underscribe,
Shall tell the vicar; but a special gentle,
That is the heir to forty marks a year,
Consorts with the small poets of the time,
Is the sole hope of his old grandmother;
That knows the law, and writes you six fair hands,
Is a fine clerk, and has his ciph'ring perfect;   60
Will take his oath o' the Greek Xenophon,
If need be, in his pocket; and can court
His mistress out of Ovid.

DAPPER   Nay, dear Captain—

FACE   Did you not tell me so?

DAPPER   Yes; but I'd ha' you
Use Master Doctor with some more respect.

FACE   Hang him, proud stag, with his broad velvet head!—

41 **angels** gold coins worth about 10s 51 **Clim . . . Claribels** heroes
of ballad and romance 52 **five . . . flush** winning hands in the game
of primero 55 **gentle** gentleman 59 **six fair hands** professional scribes
like Dapper cultivated several different handwritings for use in vari-
ous types of documents 61 **Xenophon** Jonson changed this from
"Testament" in the first edition to conform with the new law against
profanity

But for your sake, I'd choke ere I would change
An article of breath with such a puck-fist!
Come, let's be gone.   [*Going.*]

SUBTLE   Pray you, le' me speak with you.
DAPPER   His worship calls you, Captain.
70 FACE   I am sorry
I e'er embark'd myself in such a business.
DAPPER   Nay, good sir; he did call you.
FACE   Will he take then?
SUBTLE   First, hear me—
FACE   Not a syllable, 'less you take.
SUBTLE   Pray ye, sir—
FACE   Upon no terms but an *assumpsit*.
SUBTLE   Your humour must be law.
                              He takes the money.
FACE   Why now, sir, talk.
Now I dare hear you with mine honour. Speak.
So may this gentleman too.
SUBTLE   Why, sir—
              [*Offering to whisper to Face.*]
FACE   No whisp'ring.
SUBTLE   'Fore heav'n, you do not apprehend the loss
You do yourself in this.
FACE   Wherein? for what?
80 SUBTLE   Marry, to be so importunate for one
That, when he has it, will undo you all:
He'll win up all the money i' the town.
FACE   How!
SUBTLE   Yes, and blow up gamester after gamester,
As they do crackers in a puppet-play.
If I do give him a familiar,
Give you him all you play for; never set him,
For he will have it.
FACE   You're mistaken, Doctor.
Why, he does ask one but for cups and horses,
A rifling fly; none o' your great familiars.
90 DAPPER   Yes, Captain, I would have it for all games.
SUBTLE   I told you so.
FACE [*Taking* DAPPER *aside*.]   'Slight, that's a new business!

68 **puck-fist** braggart (literally, puff-ball) 74 **assumpsit** He has taken
the money and undertaken the affair (legal term). 84 **crackers** fire-
crackers 86 **set him** bet against him

I understood you, a tame bird, to fly
Twice in a term, or so, on Friday nights,
When you had left the office, for a nag
Of forty or fifty shillings.

   DAPPER   Ay, 'tis true, sir;
But I do think, now, I shall leave the law,
And therefore—

   FACE   Why, this changes quite the case!
D' you think that I dare move him?

   DAPPER   If you please, sir;
All's one to him, I see.

   FACE   What! for that money?   **100**
I cannot with my conscience; nor should you
Make the request, methinks.

   DAPPER   No, sir, I mean
To add consideration.

   FACE   Why, then, sir,
I'll try. [*Goes to* SUBTLE.]   Say that it were for all games,
Doctor?

   SUBTLE   I say then, not a mouth shall eat for him
At any ordinary, but o' the score,
That is a gaming mouth, conceive me.

   FACE   Indeed!

   SUBTLE   He'll draw you all the treasure of the realm,
If it be set him.

   FACE   Speak you this from art?   **110**

   SUBTLE   Ay, sir, and reason too, the ground of art.
He's o' the only best complexion,
The queen of Faery loves.

   FACE   What! Is he?

   SUBTLE   Peace.
He'll overhear you. Sir, should she but see him—

   FACE   What?

   SUBTLE   Do not you tell him.

   FACE   Will he win at cards too?

   SUBTLE   The spirits of dead Holland, living Isaac,
You'd swear, were in him; such a vigorous luck
As cannot be resisted. 'Slight, he'll put
Six o' your gallants to a cloak, indeed.

   FACE   A strange success, that some man shall be born to!   **120**

---

106 ordinary tavern o' the score on credit 116 Holland . . . Isaac two
card-sharpers(?) 119 put . . . cloak force five out of six gamblers to
pawn their cloaks

SUBTLE   He hears you, man—
DAPPER   Sir, I'll not be ingrateful.
FACE   Faith, I have a confidence in his good nature:
You hear, he says he will not be ingrateful.
SUBTLE   Why, as you please; my venture follows yours.
FACE   Troth, do it, Doctor; think him trusty, and make
him.
He may make us both happy in an hour;
Win some five thousand pound, and send us two on't.
DAPPER   Believe it, and I will, sir.
FACE   And you shall, sir.
You have heard all?   FACE *takes him aside.*
130   DAPPER   No, what was't? Nothing, I, sir.
FACE   Nothing?
DAPPER   A little, sir.
FACE   Well, a rare star
Reign'd at your birth.
DAPPER   At mine, sir! No.
FACE   The Doctor
Swears that you are—
SUBTLE   Nay, Captain, you'll tell all now.
FACE   Allied to the queen of Faery.
DAPPER   Who! That I am?
Believe it, no such matter—
FACE   Yes, and that
You were born with a caul o' your head.
DAPPER   Who says so?
FACE   Come,
You know it well enough, though you dissemble it.
DAPPER   I' fac, I do not; you are mistaken.
FACE   How!
Swear by your fac, and in a thing so known
140   Unto the Doctor? How shall we, sir, trust you
I' the other matter? Can we ever think,
When you have won five or six thousand pound,
You'll send us shares in 't, by this rate?
DAPPER   By Jove, sir,
I'll win ten thousand pound, and send you half.
I' fac's no oath.
SUBTLE   No, no, he did but jest.
FACE   Go to. Go thank the Doctor. He's your friend,
To take it so.
139 fac faith

DAPPER   I thank his worship.

FACE   So!

Another angel.

DAPPER   Must I?

FACE   Must you! 'Slight,

What else is thanks? Will you be trivial?—

        [DAPPER *gives him the money*.] Doctor,

When must he come for his familiar?   150

DAPPER   Shall I not ha' it with me?

SUBTLE   O, good sir!

There must a world of ceremonies pass;

You must be bath'd and fumigated first;

Besides, the queen of Faery does not rise

Till it be noon.

FACE   Not if she danc'd to-night.

SUBTLE   And she must bless it.

FACE   Did you never see

Her Royal Grace yet?

DAPPER   Whom?

FACE   Your aunt of Faery?

SUBTLE   Not since she kiss'd him in the cradle, **Captain**;

I can resolve you that.

FACE   Well, see her Grace,

Whate'er it cost you, for a thing that I know.   160

It will be somewhat hard to compass; but

However, see her. You are made, believe it,

If you can see her. Her Grace is a lone woman,

And very rich; and if she take a fancy,

She will do strange things. See her, at any hand.

'Slid, she may hap to leave you all she has!

It is the Doctor's fear.

DAPPER   How will't be done, then?

FACE   Let me alone, take you no thought. Do you

But say to me, "Captain, I'll see her Grace."

DAPPER   "Captain. I'll see her Grace."

FACE   Enough.   *One knocks without.*

SUBTLE   Who's there?   170

Anon!— [*Aside to Face.*] Conduct him forth by the back

way.—

Sir, against one o'clock prepare yourself;

Till when, you must be fasting; only, take

Three drops of vinegar in at your nose,

₁55 to-night last night **168 let me alone** leave it to me

Two at your mouth, and one at either ear;
Then bathe your fingers' ends and wash your eyes,
To sharpen your five senses, and cry "hum"
Thrice, and then "buz" as often; and then come.   [*Exit.*]

  FACE Can you remember this?
180 DAPPER   I warrant you.
  FACE Well then, away. 'Tis but your bestowing
Some twenty nobles 'mong her Grace's servants,
And put on a clean shirt. You do not know
What grace her Grace may do you in clean linen.

    [*Exeunt* FACE *and* DAPPER.]

SCENE III

[SUBTLE *within, as if to other clients.*] Come in! Good
    wives, I pray you, forbear me now;
Troth, I can do you no good till afternoon.—

   [*Enter* SUBTLE, *followed by* DRUGGER.]

What is your name, say you? Abel Drugger?
  DRUGGER Yes, sir.
  SUBTLE A seller of tobacco?
  DRUGGER   Yes, sir.
  SUBTLE   Umph!
Free of the Grocers?
  DRUGGER   Ay, an't please you.
  SUBTLE   Well—
Your business, Abel?
  DRUGGER   This, an't please your worship:
I am a young beginner, and am building
Of a new shop, an't like your worship, just
10 At corner of a street.—Here's the plot on 't—
And I would know by art, sir, of your worship,
Which way I should make my door, by necromancy,
And where my shelves; and which should be for boxes,
And which for pots. I would be glad to thrive, sir;
And I was wish'd to your worship by a gentleman,
One Captain Face, that says you know men's planets,
And their good angels, and their bad.
  SUBTLE   I do,

182 **nobles** coins worth 6s. 8d 1 **forbear** spare 6 **Free . . . Grocers** a
member of the Grocers' Company

If I do see 'em—

[*Enter* FACE]

FACE   What! my honest Abel?
Thou art well met here.
    DRUGGER   Troth, sir, I was speaking,
Just as your worship came here, of your worship.   20
I pray you, speak for me to Master Doctor.
    FACE   He shall do anything. Doctor, do you hear?
This is my friend, Abel, an honest fellow;
He lets me have good tobacco, and he does not
Sophisticate it with sack-lees or oil,
Nor washes it in muscadel and grains,
Nor buries it in gravel, under ground,
Wrapp'd up in greasy leather, or piss'd clouts,
But keeps it in fine lily pots that, open'd,
Smell like conserve of roses, or French beans.   30
He has his maple block, his silver tongs,
Winchester pipes, and fire of juniper:
A neat, spruce, honest fellow, and no goldsmith.
    SUBTLE   He's a fortunate fellow, that I am sure on.
    FACE   Already, sir, ha' you found it? Lo thee, Abel!
    SUBTLE   And in right way toward riches—
    FACE   Sir!
    SUBTLE   This summer
He will be of the clothing of his company,
And next spring call'd to the scarlet, spend what he can.
    FACE   What, and so little beard?
    SUBTLE   Sir, you must think,
He may have a receipt to make hair come.   40
But he'll be wise, preserve his youth, and fine for 't;
His fortune looks for him another way.
    FACE   'Slid, Doctor, how canst thou know this so soon?
I am amus'd at that.
    SUBTLE   By a rule, Captain,
In metoposcopy, which I do work by;

---

26 **grains** a kind of spice 29 **lily pots** ornamental jars 32 **maple** . . .
juniper Tobacconists provided facilities for smoking in their shops.
The tobacco was shredded on a maple block, and pipes were lighted from
coals of slow-burning juniper wood held in silver tongs. 33 **goldsmith**
usurer 37 **be** . . . **clothing** wear the livery 38 **call'd** . . . **scarlet** made
sheriff 41 **fine** pay the fine for declining to serve as sheriff 44 **amus'd**
amazed, made to muse 45 **metoposcopy** a branch of physiognomy

A certain star i' the forehead, which you see not.
Your chestnut or your olive-colour'd face
Does never fail, and your long ear doth promise.
I knew 't by certain spots, too, in his teeth,
50 And on the nail of his mercurial finger.
    FACE   Which finger's that?
    SUBTLE   His little finger. Look.
You were born upon a Wednesday?
    DRUGGER   Yes, indeed, sir.
    SUBTLE   The thumb, in chiromancy, we give Venus;
The forefinger to Jove; the midst to Saturn;
The ring to Sol; the least to Mercury,
Who was the lord, sir, of his horoscope,
His house of life being Libra; which foreshow'd
He should be a merchant, and should trade with balance.
    FACE   Why, this is strange! Is't not, honest Nab?
60   SUBTLE   There is a ship now coming from Ormus,
That shall yield him such a commodity
Of drugs—This is the west, and this the south?
                [*Pointing to the plan.*]
    DRUGGER   Yes, sir.
    SUBTLE   And those are your two sides?
    DRUGGER   Ay, sir.
    SUBTLE   Make me your door then, south; your broad side,
west;
And on the east side of your shop, aloft,
Write Mathlai, Tarmiel, and Baraborat;
Upon the north part, Rael, Velel, Thiel.
They are the names of those Mercurial spirits
That do fright flies from boxes.
    DRUGGER   Yes, sir.
70   SUBTLE   And
Beneath your threshold, bury me a loadstone
To draw in gallants that wear spurs; the rest,
They'll seem to follow.
    FACE   That's a secret, Nab!
    SUBTLE   And, on your stall, a puppet, with a vice,
And a court-fucus, to call city-dames.
You shall deal much with minerals.
    DRUGGER   Sir, I have,

68 **Mathlai . . . Thiel** names of spirits in Pietro d'Abano's *Elementa Magica* 73 **seem** think it seemly 74 **puppet . . . vice** mechanical figure 75 **court-fucus** cosmetic

At home, already—

SUBTLE   Ay, I know, you've arsenic,
Vitriol, sal-tartar, argaile, alkali,
Cinoper: I know all.—This fellow, Captain,
Will come, in time, to be a great distiller,   80
And give a say—I will not say directly,
But very fair—at the philosopher's stone.

FACE   Why, how now, Abel! is this true?

DRUGGER [*Aside to* FACE.]   Good Captain,
What must I give?

FACE   Nay, I'll not counsel thee.
Thou hear'st what wealth (he says, spend what thou canst)
Th' art like to come to.

DRUGGER   I would gi' him a crown.

FACE   A crown! and toward such a fortune? Heart,
Thou shalt rather gi' him thy shop. No gold about thee?

DRUGGER Yes, I have a portague, I ha' kept this half-year.

FACE   Out on thee, Nab! 'Slight, there was such an offer— 90
Shalt keep 't no longer, I'll gi' it him for thee. Doctor,
Nab prays your worship to drink this, and swears
He will appear more grateful, as your skill
Does raise him in the world.

DRUGGER   I would entreat
Another favour of his worship.

FACE   What is't, Nab?

DRUGGER But to look over, sir, my almanac,
And cross out my ill-days, that I may neither
Bargain, nor trust upon them.

FACE   That he shall, Nab.
Leave it, it shall be done, 'gainst afternoon.

SUBTLE   And a direction for his shelves.

FACE   Now, Nab,   100
Art thou well pleas'd, Nab?

DRUGGER 'Thank, sir, both your worships.

FACE   Away.   [*Exit* DRUGGER.]
Why, now, you smoky persecutor of nature!
Now do you see, that something's to be done,
Beside your beech-coal, and your cor'sive waters,
Your crosslets, crucibles, and cucurbites?
You must have stuff brought home to you, to work on!

81 **give a say** make an attempt 89 **portague** a gold coin worth about $18
97 **ill-days** unlucky days 106 **cor'sive** corrosive 107 **crosslets, cucurbites**
glass vessels used in alchemy

And yet you think I am at no expense
110 In searching out these veins, then following 'em,
Then trying 'em out. 'Fore God, my intelligence
Costs me more money than my share oft comes to,
In these rare works.

    SUBTLE   You're pleasant, sir.—How now!

SCENE IV

[*Enter* DOL COMMON.]

    SUBTLE   What says my dainty Dolkin?
    DOL COMMON   Yonder fish-wife
Will not away. And there's your giantess,
The bawd of Lambeth.
    SUBTLE   Heart, I cannot speak with 'em.
    DOL COMMON   Not afore night, I have told 'em in a voice,
Thorough the trunk, like one of your familiars.
But I have spied Sir Epicure Mammon—
    SUBTLE   Where?
    DOL COMMON   Coming along, at far end of the lane,
Slow of his feet, but earnest of his tongue
To one that's with him.
    SUBTLE   Face, go you and shift.
10 Dol, you must presently make ready too.

                                       [*Exit* FACE.]

    DOL COMMON   Why, what's the matter?
    SUBTLE   O, I did look for him
With the sun's rising: marvel he could sleep!
This is the day I am to perfect for him
The magisterium, our great work, the stone;
And yield it, made, into his hands; of which
He has, this month, talk'd as he were possess'd.
And now he's dealing pieces on 't away.
Methinks I see him ent'ring ordinaries,
Dispensing for the pox, and plaguy houses,
20 Reaching his dose, walking Moorfields for lepers,
And off'ring citizens' wives pomander-bracelets
As his preservative, made of the elixir;

5 **trunk** speaking-tube 9 **shift** change your cosutme 21 **pomander** a
perfume ball supposed to protect the wearer from infection

Searching the 'spital, to make old bawds young;
And the highways, for beggars to make rich.
I see no end of his labours. He will make
Nature asham'd of her long sleep; when art,
Who's but a step-dame, shall do more than she,
In her best love to mankind, ever could.
If his dream last, he'll turn the age to gold.

                                              [*Exeunt.*]

23 **'spital** hospital

Act II

[*Enter* SIR EPICURE MAMMON *and* SURLY.]

[MAMMON]   Come on, sir. Now you set your foot on shore
In *Novo Orbe;* here's the rich Peru,
And there within, sir, are the golden mines,
Great Solomon's Ophir! He was sailing to 't
Three years, but we have reach'd it in ten months.
This is the day wherein, to all my friends,
I will pronounce the happy word, *Be rich;*
This day you shall be spectatissimi.
You shall no more deal with the hollow die,
10   Or the frail card; no more be at charge of keeping
The livery-punk for the young heir, that must
Seal, at all hours, in his shirt: no more,
If he deny, ha' him beaten to 't, as he is
That brings him the commodity; no more
Shall thirst of satin, or the covetous hunger
Of velvet entrails for a rude-spun cloak,
To be display'd at Madam Augusta's, make
The sons of Sword and Hazard fall before
The golden calf, and on their knees, whole nights,
20 Commit idolatry with wine and trumpets,
Or go a-feasting after drum and ensign.
No more of this. You shall start up young viceroys,
And have your punks and punkettees, my Surly.
And unto thee I speak it first, *be rich.*
Where is my Subtle there? Within, ho!
    [FACE *within.*]   Sir,
He'll come to you by and by.
    MAMMON   That's his fire-drake,
His Lungs, his Zephyrus, he that puffs his coals,

2 **Novo Orbe** the New World 8 **spectatissimi** most gazed at 9 **hollow die** loaded dice 11 **livery-punk** prostitute-accomplice of a swindler 12 **Seal** seal a bond, in favor of the swindlers 14 **commodity** Elizabethan loan sharks often gave borrowers merchandise, or "commodity," instead of cash. The borrower then found that he must sell the goods at a heavy loss 16 **entrails** lining 17 **Madam Augusta** mistress of a brothel(?) 26 **fire-drake** dragon

Till he firk nature up, in her own center.
You are not faithful, sir. This night I'll change
All that is metal in my house to gold,   30
And, early in the morning, will I send
To all the plumbers and the pewterers
And buy their tin and lead up; and to Lothbury
For all the copper.

    SURLY   What, and turn that, too?

    MAMMON Yes, and I'll purchase Devonshire and Cornwall,
And make them perfect Indies! You admire now?

    SURLY No, faith.

    MAMMON But when you see th' effects of the Great Med-
'cine,
Of which one part projected on a hundred   40
Of Mercury, or Venus, or the Moon,
Shall turn it to as many of the Sun;
Nay, to a thousand, so *ad infinitum:*
You will believe me.

    SURLY   Yes, when I see 't, I will.
But if my eyes do cozen me so, and I
Giving 'em no occasion, sure I'll have
A whore, shall piss 'em out next day.

    MAMMON   Ha! why?
Do you think I fable with you? I assure you,
He that has once the flower of the sun,
The perfect ruby, which we call elixir,   50
Not only can do that, but by its virtue,
Can confer honour, love, respect, long life;
Give safety, valour, yea, and victory,
To whom he will. In eight-and-twenty days,
I'll make an old man of fourscore a child.

    SURLY No doubt: he's that already.

    MAMMON   Nay, I mean,
Restore his years, renew him, like an eagle,
To the fifth age; make him get sons and daughters,
Young giants; as our philosophers have done,
The ancient patriarchs, afore the flood,   60
But taking, once a week, on a knife's point,
The quantity of a grain of mustard of it;

28 **firk** stir 29 **faithful** a believer 33 **Lothbury** a street in London in-
habited largely by coppersmiths 35 **Devonshire, Cornwall** counties noted
for tin and copper mines 36 **admire** wonder 41 **Venus** copper **Moon**
silver 42 **Sun** gold

Become stout Marses, and beget young Cupids.
   SURLY   The decay'd vestals of Pickt-hatch would thank you,
That keep the fire alive there.
   MAMMON   'Tis the secret
Of nature naturiz'd 'gainst all infections,
Cures all diseases coming of all causes;
A month's grief in a day, a year's in twelve;
70 And, of what age soever, in a month,
Past all the doses of your drugging doctors.
I'll undertake, withal, to fright the plague
Out o' the kingdom in three months.
   SURLY   And I'll
Be bound, the players shall sing your praises then,
Without their poets.
   MAMMON   Sir, I'll do 't. Meantime,
I'll give away so much unto my man,
Shall serve th' whole city with preservative
Weekly; each house his dose, and at the rate—
   SURLY   As he that built the Water-work does with water?
   MAMMON   You are incredulous.
80   SURLY   Faith, I have a humour,
I would not willingly be gull'd. Your stone
Cannot transmute me.
   MAMMON   Pertinax Surly,
Will you believe antiquity? Records?
I'll show you a book where Moses, and his sister,
And Solomon have written of the art;
Ay, and a treatise penn'd by Adam—
   SURLY   How!
   MAMMON   O' the philosopher's stone, and in High Dutch.
   SURLY   Did Adam write, sir, in High Dutch?
   MAMMON   He did;
Which proves it was the primitive tongue.
   SURLY   What paper?

64 Pickt-hatch a resort of prostitutes and pick-pockets 73 'Tis the secret
... months These were familiar claims of alchemists, not Jonson's invention 74 players Since the theatres were closed by law during visitations
of the plague, the players lost their livelihood. They were therefore especially concerned about the plague 79 Water-work a pumping station
built in 1594 to supply water from the Thames 88 High Dutch These
and most of the following absurdities can be found in the crack-pot
literature of the time. Jonson satirizes; he does not invent.

MAMMON   On cedar board.

SURLY   O that, indeed, they say,   90
Will last 'gainst worms.

MAMMON   'Tis like your Irish wood
'Gainst cobwebs. I have a piece of Jason's fleece too,
Which was no other than a book of alchemy,
Writ in large sheepskin, a good fat ram-vellum.
Such was Pythagoras' thigh, Pandora's tub,
And all that fable of Medea's charms,
The manner of our work; the bulls, our furnace,
Still breathing fire; our *argent-vive,* the dragon;
The dragon's teeth, mercury sublimate,
That keeps the whiteness, hardness, and the biting;   100
And they are gather'd into Jason's helm,
Th' alembic, and then sow'd in Mars his field,
And thence sublim'd so often, till they're fix'd.
Both this, th' Hesperian garden, Cadmus' story,
Jove's shower, the boon of Midas, Argus' eyes,
Boccace his Demogorgon, thousands more,
All abstract riddles of our stone.—How now!

Scene II

[Enter FACE, *now disguised as* SUBTLE's *laboratory assistant
and called* LUNGS *or* ULEN SPIEGEL.]

[MAMMON]   Do we succeed? Is our day come? And
holds it?

FACE   The evening will set red upon you, sir;
You have colour for it, crimson: the red ferment
Has done his office; three hours hence prepare you
To see projection.

MAMMON   Pertinax, my Surly,
Again I say to thee, aloud, *be rich.*
This day thou shalt have ingots; and tomorrow
Give lords th' affront.—Is it, my Zephyrus, right?
Blushes the bolt's-head?

FACE   Like a wench with child, sir,   10
That were but now discover'd to her master.

MAMMON   Excellent witty Lungs!—My only care is

98 **argent-vive** quicksilver 106 **Demogorgon** the ancestor of all the gods
in Boccaccio's *Genealogia Deorum* 10 **bolt's-head** a kind of flask

Where to get stuff enough now, to project on;
This town will not half serve me.

FACE   No, sir? Buy
The covering off o' churches.

    MAMMON   That's true.

    FACE   Yes.
Let 'em stand bare, as do their auditory;
Or cap 'em new with shingles.

    MAMMON   No, good thatch:
Thatch will lie light upo' the rafters, Lungs.
Lungs, I will manumit thee from the furnace;

20 I will restore thee thy complexion, Puff,
Lost in the embers; and repair this brain,
Hurt wi' the fume o' the metals.

    FACE   I have blown, sir,
Hard, for your worship; thrown by many a coal,
When 't was not beech; weigh'd those I put in, just,
To keep your heat still even. These blear'd eyes
Have wak'd to read your several colours, sir,
Of the pale citron, the green lion, the crow,
The peacock's tail, the plumed swan.

    MAMMON   And lastly,
Thou hast descried the flower, the *sanguis agni*?

    FACE   Yes, sir.

    MAMMON   Where's master?

30 FACE   At's prayers, sir, he;
Good man, he's doing his devotions
For the success.

    MAMMON   Lungs, I will set a period
To all thy labours; thou shalt be the master
Of my seraglio.

    FACE   Good, sir.

    MAMMON   But do you hear?
I'll geld you, Lungs.

    FACE   Yes, sir.

    MAMMON   For I do mean
To have a list of wives and concubines
Equal with Solomon, who had the stone
Alike with me; and I will make me a back
With the elixir, that shall be as tough

40 As Hercules, to encounter fifty a night.—

24 **just** with accuracy 26 **colours** indications of the progress of the
operation

Th'art sure thou saw'st it blood?
   FACE   Both blood and spirit, sir.
   MAMMON   I will have all my beds blown up, not stuff'd:
Down is too hard; and then, mine oval room
Fill'd with such pictures as Tiberius took
From Elephantis, and dull Aretine
But coldly imitated. Then, my glasses
Cut in more subtle angles, to disperse
And multiply the figures, as I walk
Naked between my succubæ. My mists
I'll have of perfume, vapour'd 'bout the room,   50
To lose our selves in; and my baths, like pits
To fall into; from whence we will come forth,
And roll us dry in gossamer and roses.—
Is it arrived at ruby?—Where I spy
A wealthy citizen, or rich lawyer,
Have a sublim'd pure wife, unto that fellow
I'll send a thousand pound to be my cuckold.
   FACE   And I shall carry it?
   MAMMON   No, I'll ha' no bawds
But fathers and mothers: they will do it best,
Best of all others. And my flatterers   60
Shall be the pure, and gravest of divines
That I can get for money. My mere fools,
Eloquent burgesses, and then my poets
The same that writ so subtly of the fart,
Whom I will entertain still for that subject.
The few that would give out themselves to be
Court-and town-stallions, and, each-where, bely
Ladies who are known most innocent, for them,—
These will I beg, to make me eunuchs of,
And they shall fan me with ten estrich tails   70
Apiece, made in a plume to gather wind.
We will be brave, Puff, now we ha' the med'cine.
My meat shall all come in, in Indian shells,
Dishes of agate set in gold, and studded
With emeralds, sapphires, hyacinths, and rubies.
The tongues of carps, dormice, and camels' heels,
Boil'd i' the spirit of Sol, and dissolv'd pearl

45 **Elephantis, Aretine** both wrote verses to accompany lewd pictures
49 **succubæ** concubines 77 **spirit of Sol** gold **Boil'd . . .** epilepsy From
Lampridius's life of Heliogabalus, Jonson's source for most of these
delicacies

(Apicius' diet, 'gainst the epilepsy):
And I will eat these broths with spoons of amber,
80 Headed with diamond and carbuncle.
My foot-boy shall eat pheasants, calver'd salmons,
Knots, godwits, lampreys. I myself will have
The beards of barbels serv'd instead of salads;
Oil'd mushrooms; and the swelling unctuous paps
Of a fat pregnant sow, newly cut off,
Dress'd with an exquisite and poignant sauce;
For which, I'll say unto my cook, *There's gold;*
Go forth, and be a knight.

    FACE   Sir, I'll go look
A little, how it heightens.   [*Exit.*]

    MAMMON   Do.—My shirts
90 I'll have of taffeta-sarsnet, soft and light
As cobwebs; and for all my other raiment,
It shall be such as might provoke the Persian,
Were he to teach the world riot anew.
My gloves of fishes and birds' skins, perfum'd
With gums of paradise, and Eastern air—

    SURLY   And do you think to have the stone with this?
    MAMMON   No, I do think t' have all this with the stone.
    SURLY   Why, I have heard he must be *homo frugi,*
A pious, holy, and religious man,
100 One free from mortal sin, a very virgin.

    MAMMON   That makes it, sir; he is so. But I buy it;
My venture brings it me. He, honest wretch,
A notable, superstitious, good soul,
Has worn his knees bare and his slippers bald
With prayer and fasting for it. And, sir, let him
Do it alone, for me, still. Here he comes.
Not a profane word afore him; 't is poison.—

81 **calver'd** an elaborate method of preparing fish, now unknown
82 **Knots** a kind of snipe **godwits** marsh birds 83 **barbels** fresh-water
fish 88 **knight** a sly dig at King James' wholesale creation of unde-
serving knights 90 **taffeta-sarsnet** a fine silk 98 **homo frugi** a temperate
man

Scene III

[*Enter* SUBTLE.]

MAMMON Good morrow, father.

SUBTLE Gentle son, good morrow,
And to your friend there. What is he is with you?

MAMMON An heretic, that I did bring along,
In hope, sir, to convert him.

SUBTLE Son, I doubt
You're covetous, that thus you meet your time
I' the just point, prevent your day at morning.
This argues something worthy of a fear
Of importune and carnal appetite.
Take heed you do not cause the blessing leave you,
With your ungovern'd haste. I should be sorry   10
To see my labours, now e'en at perfection,
Got by long watching and large patience,
Not prosper where my love and zeal hath plac'd 'em:
Which (heaven I call to witness, with your self,
To whom I have pour'd my thoughts) in all my ends,
Have look'd no way, but unto public good,
To pious uses, and dear charity,
Now grown a prodigy with men. Wherein
If you, my son, should now prevaricate,
And to your own particular lusts employ   20
So great and catholic a bliss, be sure
A curse will follow, yea, and overtake
Your subtle and most secret ways.

MAMMON I know, sir;
You shall not need to fear me; I but come
To ha' you confute this gentleman.

SURLY Who is,
Indeed, sir, somewhat costive of belief
Toward your stone; would not be gull'd.

SUBTLE Well, son,
All that I can convince him in, is this,
The work is done, bright Sol is in his robe.
We have a med'cine of the triple soul,   30
The glorified spirit. Thanks be to heaven,
And make us worthy of it!—

4 doubt fear 6 just exact prevent anticipate 30 med'cine . . . spirit *i.e.*
the philosopher's stone

[*Calling to* FACE.]
Ulen Spiegel!

FACE [*Within.*]   Anon, sir.

SUBTLE   Look well to the register,
And let your heat still lessen by degrees,
To the aludels.

FACE [Within.]   Yes, sir.

SUBTLE   Did you look
O' the bolt's-head yet?

FACE [Within.]   Which? On D, sir?

SUBTLE   Ay;
What's the complexion?

FACE [Within.]   Whitish.

SUBTLE   Infuse vinegar,
40 To draw his volatile substance and his tincture,
And let the water in glass E be filt'red,
And put into the gripe's egg. Lute him well;
And leave him clos'd *in balneo*.

FACE [*Within.*]   I will, sir.

SURLY [*Aside.*]   What a brave language here is! next to
canting!

SUBTLE   I have another work you never saw, son,
That three days since passed the philosopher's wheel,
In the lent heat of Athanor; and 's become
Sulphur o' Nature.

MAMMON   But 'tis for me?

SUBTLE   What need you?
You have enough, in that is, perfect.

50 MAMMON   O, but—

SUBTLE   Why, this is covetise!

MAMMON   No, I assure you,
I shall employ it all in pious uses,
Founding of colleges and grammar schools,
Marrying young virgins, building hospitals,
And, now and then, a church.

32 **Ulen Spiegel** Owl Glass, the rogue-hero of an old German jest-book
33 Here and in the lines following Jonson uses correctly the highly technical jargon of the alchemists to give the effect of authenticity. The original audience probably did not understand the exact meaning of the
terms, but the words at least had a more familiar sound then than now.
Cf. *Volpone*, II, ii. 122 ff. "Aludels," "gripe's egg," "Athanor," etc. are
vessels or implements used in alchemy; "lute," *"in balneo,"* "imbibition," "St. Mary's bath," *"lac virginis,"* "calx," etc., are processes or
materials employed in the science 45 **canting** thieves' slang 51 **covetise**
covetousness

[*Enter* FACE.]

SUBTLE　　　　　　　　How now!

FACE　　　　　　　　　　　Sir, please you,

Shall I not change the filter?

SUBTLE　　　　　　　Marry, yes;

And bring me the complexion of glass B.　　　[*Exit* FACE.]

MAMMON　Ha' you another?

SUBTLE　　　　　　　　Yes, son; were I assur'd

Your piety were firm, we would not want

The means to glorify it: but I hope the best.　　　　　　　60

I mean to tinct C in sand-heat to-morrow,

And give him imbibition.

MAMMON　　　　　　Of white oil?

SUBTLE　No, sir, of red. F is come over the helm too,

I thank my maker, in St. Mary's bath,

And shows *lac virginis*. Blessed be heaven!

I sent you of his fæces there calcin'd;

Out of that calx, I ha' won the salt of mercury.

MAMMON　By pouring on your rectified water?

SUBTLE　Yes, and reverberating in Athanor.

[*Re-enter* FACE.]

How now! what colour says it?

FACE　　　　　　　　The ground black, sir.　　　70

MAMMON　That's your crow's head?

SURLY　[*Aside.*]　　　　Your cock's comb's, is it not?

SUBTLE　No, 'tis not perfect. Would it were the crow!

That work wants something.

SURLY　[*Aside.*]　　　　O, I look'd for this,

The hay is a-pitching.

SUBTLE　　　　　Are you sure you loos'd 'em

I' their own menstrue?

FACE　　　　　Yes, sir, and then married 'em,

And put 'em in a bolt's-head nipp'd to digestion,

According as you bade me, when I set

The liquor of Mars to circulation

In the same heat.

SUBTLE　　　The process then was right.

FACE　Yes, by the token, sir, the retort brake,　　　80

And what was sav'd was put into the pelican,

And sign'd with Hermes' seal.

SUBTLE　　　　　　I think 't was so.

71 **cock's comb's** *i.e.*, coxcomb's, fool's

We should have a new amalgama.

    SURLY [*Aside.*]   O, this ferret
Is rank as any polecat.

    SUBTLE   But I care not;
Let him e'en die; we have enough beside,
In embrion. H has his white shirt on?

    FACE   Yes, sir,
He's ripe for inceration, he stands warm,
In his ash-fire. I would not you should let
Any die now, if I might counsel, sir,

90 For luck's sake to the rest: it is not good.

    MAMMON   He says right.

    SURLY [*Aside.*]   Ay, are you bolted?

    FACE   Nay, I know 't, sir,
I've seen th' ill fortune. What is some three ounces
Of fresh materials?

    MAMMON   Is 't no more?

    FACE   No more, sir,
Of gold, t' amalgam with some six of mercury.

    MAMMON   Away, here's money. What will serve?

    FACE   Ask him, sir.

    MAMMON   How much?

    SUBTLE   Give him nine pound; you may gi' him ten.

    SURLY [*Aside.*]   Yes, twenty, and be cozen'd; do.

    MAMMON   There 't is. [*Gives* FACE *the money.*]

100   SUBTLE   This needs not; but that you will have it so,
To see conclusions of all: for two
Of our inferior works are at fixation,
A third is in ascension. Go your ways.
Ha' you set the oil of Luna in kemia?

    FACE   Yes, sir.

    SUBTLE   And the philosopher's vinegar?

    FACE   Ay. [*Exit.*]

    SURLY [*Aside.*]   We shall have a salad!

    MAMMON   When do you make projection?

    SUBTLE   Son, be not hasty, I exalt our med'cine,
By hanging him *in balneo vaporoso,*

110 And giving him solution; then congeal him;
And then dissolve him; then again congeal him;
For look, how oft I iterate the work,
So many times I add unto his virtue.

91 **bolted** driven by the ferret into the net 104 **kemia** vessel for **distillation**

As, if at first one ounce convert a hundred,
After his second loose, he'll turn a thousand;
His third solution, ten; his fourth, a hundred;
After his fifth, a thousand thousand ounces
Of any imperfect metal, into pure
Silver or gold, in all examinations
As good as any of the natural mine.   120
Get you your stuff here against afternoon,
Your brass, your pewter, and your andirons.

MAMMON   Not those of iron?

SUBTLE   Yes, you may bring them too;
We'll change all metals.

SURLY [*Aside.*]   I believe you in that.

MAMMON   Then I may send my spits?

SUBTLE   Yes, and your racks.

SURLY   And dripping-pans, and pot-hangers, and hooks?
Shall he not?

SUBTLE   If he please.

SURLY   —To be an ass.

SUBTLE   How, sir!

MAMMON   This gent'man you must bear withal.
I told you he had no faith.

SURLY   And little hope, sir;   130
But much less charity, should I gull myself.

SUBTLE   Why, what have you observ'd, sir, in our art,
Seems so impossible?

SURLY   But your whole work, no more.
That you should hatch gold in a furnace, sir,
As they do eggs in Egypt!

SUBTLE   Sir, do you
Believe that eggs are hatch'd so?

SURLY   If I should?

SUBTLE   Why, I think that the greater miracle.
No egg but differs from a chicken more
Than metals in themselves.

SURLY   That cannot be.
The egg's ordain'd by nature to that end,   140
And is a chicken *in potentia*.

SUBTLE   The same we say of lead and other metals,
Which would be gold if they had time.

MAMMON   And that
Our art doth furder.

SUBTLE   Ay, for 't were absurd

To think that nature in the earth bred gold
Perfect i' the instant: something went before.
There must be remote matter.

    SURLY   Ay, what is that?

    SUBTLE Marry, we say—

    MAMMON Ay, now it heats: stand, father,
Pound him to dust.

150   SUBTLE   It is, of the one part,
A humid exhalation, which we call
Materia liquida, or the unctuous water;
On th' other part, a certain crass and viscous
Portion of earth; both which, concorporate,
Do make the elementary matter of gold;
Which is not yet *propria materia,*
But common to all metals and all stones.
For, where it is forsaken of that moisture,
And hath more dryness, it becomes a stone;
160 Where it retains more of the humid fatness,
It turns to sulphur, or to quicksilver,
Who are the parents of all other metals.
Nor can this remote matter suddenly
Progress so from extreme unto extreme,
As to grow gold, and leap o'er all the means.
Nature doth first beget th' imperfect, then
Proceeds she to the perfect. Of that airy
And oily water, mercury is engend'red;
Sulphur o' the fat and earthy part; the one,
170 Which is the last, supplying the place of male,
The other of the female, in all metals.
Some do believe hermaphrodeity,
That both do act and suffer. But these two
Make the rest ductile, malleable, extensive.
And even in gold they are; for we do find
Seeds of them by our fire, and gold in them;
And can produce the species of each metal
More perfect thence, than nature doth in earth.
Beside, who doth not see in daily practice
180 Art can beget bees, hornets, beetles, wasps,
Out of the carcases and dung of creatures;
Yea, scorpions of an herb, being rightly plac'd?
And these are living creatures, far more perfect
And excellent than metals.

    165 **means** intermediate stages

MAMMON   Well said, father!
Nay, if he take you in hand, sir, with an argument,
He'll bray you in a mortar.
        SURLY   Pray you, sir, stay.
Rather than I'll be bray'd, sir, I'll believe
That Alchemy is a pretty kind of game,
Somewhat like tricks o' the cards, to cheat a man
With charming.
        SUBTLE   Sir?
        SURLY   What else are all your terms,   190
Whereon no one o' your writers 'grees with other?
Of your elixir, your *lac virginis,*
Your stone, your med'cine, and your chrysosperm,
Your sal, your sulphur, and your mercury,
Your oil of height, your tree of life, your blood,
Your marchesite, your tutie, your magnesia,
Your toad, your crow, your dragon, and your panther,
Your sun, your moon, your firmament, your adrop,
Your lato, azoch, zernich, chibrit, heautarit,
And then your red man, and your white woman,   200
With all your broths, your menstrues, and materials
Of piss and egg-shells, women's terms, man's blood,
Hair o' the head, burnt clouts, chalk, merds, and clay,
Powder of bones, scalings of iron, glass,
And worlds of other strange ingredients,
Would burst a man to name?
        SUBTLE   And all these, nam'd,
Intending but one thing; which art our writers
Us'd to obscure their art.
        MAMMON   Sir, so I told him—
Because the simple idiot should not learn it,
And make it vulgar.
        SUBTLE   Was not all the knowledge   210
Of the Egyptians writ in mystic symbols?
Speak not the Scriptures oft in parables?
Are not the choicest fables of the poets,
That were the fountains and first springs of wisdom,
Wrapp'd in perplexed allegories?
        MAMMON   I urg'd that,
And clear'd to him, that Sisyphus was damn'd
To roll the ceaseless stone, only because
He would have made ours common.

190 All Surly's terms are found in contemporary alchemical treatises

[DOL *appears at the door*.]

                  Who is this?

SUBTLE   God's precious!—What do you mean? Go in,
220 good lady,
Let me entreat you. [DOL *retires*.]—[*Calling*.] Where's this
    varlet?

               [*Re-enter* FACE.]

FACE   Sir.

SUBTLE   You very knave! do you use me thus?

FACE   Wherein, sir?

SUBTLE   Go in and see, you traitor. Go!

               [*Exit* FACE.]

MAMMON   Who is it, sir?

SUBTLE   Nothing, sir; nothing.

MAMMON   What's the matter, good sir?
I have not seen you thus distemp'red: who is 't?

SUBTLE   All arts have still had, sir, their adversaries;
But ours the most ignorant.—

             FACE *returns*.

               What now?

FACE   'T was not my fault, sir; she would speak with you.
230 SUBTLE   Would she, sir! Follow me.   [*Exit*.]

MAMMON [*Stopping him*.]   Stay, Lungs.

FACE   I dare not, sir.

MAMMON   How! pray thee, stay.

FACE   She's mad, sir, and sent hither—

MAMMON   Stay, man; what is she?

FACE   A lord's sister, sir.
He'll be mad too—

MAMMON   I warrant thee.—Why sent hither?

FACE   Sir, to be cur'd.

SUBTLE [*Within*.]   Why, rascal!

FACE   Lo, you!—here, sir!
                         He goes out.

MAMMON   'Fore God, a Bradamante, a brave piece.
240 SURLY   Heart, this is a bawdy-house! I'll be burnt else.

MAMMON   O, by this light, no! Do not wrong him. He's
Too scrupulous that way; it is his vice.
No, he's a rare physician, do him right,
An excellent Paracelsian, and has done

236 warrant protect, *i.e.*, against Subtle's anger 239 **Bradamante** a heroine in Ariosto's *Orlando Furioso* 244 **Paracelsian** *i.e.*, a physician who
uses the mineral remedies of Paracelsus, instead of the vegetable remedies of Galen.

Strange cures with mineral physic. He deals all
With spirits, he; he will not hear a word
Of Galen, or his tedious recipes.—

[*Re-enter* FACE.]

                    How now, Lungs!
   FACE   Softly, sir; speak softly. I meant
To ha' told your worship all. This must not hear.
   MAMMON   No, he will not be gull'd; let him alone.   250
   FACE   Y'are very right, sir; she is a most rare scholar,
And is gone mad with studying Broughton's works.
If you but name a word touching the Hebrew,
She falls into her fit, and will discourse
So learnedly of genealogies,
As you would run mad too, to hear her, sir.
   MAMMON   How might one do t' have conference with her,
Lungs?
   FACE   O, divers have run mad upon the conference.
I do not know, sir: I am sent in haste   260
To fetch a vial.
   SURLY   Be not gull'd, Sir Mammon.
   MAMMON   Wherein? Pray ye, be patient.
   SURLY   Yes, as you are,
And trust confederate knaves and bawds and whores.
   MAMMON   You are too foul, believe it.—Come here, Ulen,
One word.
   FACE   I dare not, in good faith. [*Going.*]
   MAMMON   Stay, knave.
   FACE   He's extreme angry that you saw her, sir.
   MAMMON   Drink that. [*Gives him money.*] What is she
when she's out of her fit?
   FACE   O, the most affablest creature, sir! so merry!   270
So pleasant! She'll mount you up, like quicksilver,
Over the helm; and circulate like oil,
A very vegetal: discourse of state,
Of mathematics, bawdry, anything—
   MAMMON   Is she no way accessible? no means,
No trick to give a man a taste of her—wit—
Or so?—Ulen?
   FACE   I'll come to you again, sir. [*Exit.*]
   MAMMON   Surly, I did not think one o' your breeding

249 This Surly   252 Broughton an eccentric rabbinical scholar (d.1612)
273 vegetal animated person

Would traduce personages of worth.

280   SURLY   Sir Epicure,
Your friend to use; yet still loath to be gull'd:
I do not like your philosophical bawds.
Their stone is lechery enough to pay for,
Without this bait.

    MAMMON   Heart, you abuse yourself.
I know the lady, and her friends, and means,
The original of this disaster. Her brother
Has told me all.

    SURLY   And yet you ne'er saw her
Till now!

    MAMMON   O yes, but I forgot. I have, believe it,
290 One o' the treacherous'st memories, I do think,
Of all minkind.

    SURLY   What call you her brother?
    MAMMON   My lord—
He wi' not have his name known, now I think on't.

    SURLY   A very treacherous memory!
    MAMMON   O' my faith—
    SURLY   Tut, if you ha' it not about you, pass it
Till we meet next.

    MAMMON   Nay, by this hand, 'tis true.
He's one I honour, and my noble friend;
And I respect his house.

    SURLY   Heart! can it be
That a grave sir, a rich, that has no need,
A wise sir, too, at other times, should thus,
300 With his own oaths and arguments make hard means
To gull himself? An this be your elixir,
Your *lapis mineralis,* and your lunary,
Give me your honest trick yet at primero,
Or gleek, and take your *lutum sapientis,*
Your *menstruum simplex!* I'll have gold before you,
And with less danger of the quicksilver,
Or the hot sulphur.

             [*Re-enter* FACE.]

    FACE   Here's one from Captain Face, sir,

302 **lapis mineralis** philosopher's stone **lunary** moonwort 303 **primero,
gleek** card games 304 **lutum sapientis** philosopher's clay 305 **menstruum
simplex** simple dissolvent 306 **quicksilver** . . . **sulphur** the usual treat-
ments for venereal disease 308 **Captain Face** Surly has failed to recognize
Face, the laboratory assistant, as the same man he has seen elsewhere
called Captain Face

To SURLY.

Desires you meet him i' the Temple-church,
Some half-hour hence, and upon earnest business.—   310

He whispers MAMMON.

Sir, if you please to quit us now, and come
Again within two hours, you shall have
My master busy examining o' the works;
And I will steal you in unto the party,
That you may see her converse.— [*To* SURLY.] Sir,
shall I say
You'll meet the captain's worship?
    SURLY   Sir, I will.—   [*Aside.*]
But, by attorney, and to a second purpose.
Now I am sure it is a bawdy-house;
I'll swear it, were the marshal here to thank me: 320
The naming this commander doth confirm it.
Don Face! why he's the most authentic dealer
I' these commodities, the superintendent
To all the quainter traffickers in town!
He is the visitor, and does appoint
Who lies with whom, and at what hour; what price;
Which gown, and in what smock; what fall; what tire.
Him will I prove, by a third person, to find
The subtleties of this dark labyrinth:
Which if I do discover, dear Sir Mammon,   330
You'll give your poor friend leave, though no philosopher,
To laugh; for you that are, 't is thought, shall weep.
    FACE   Sir, he does pray you'll not forget.
    SURLY   I will not, sir.
Sir Epicure, I shall leave you?   [*Exit.*]
    MAMMON   I follow you straight.
    FACE   But do so, good sir, to avoid suspicion.
This gent'man has a parlous head.
    MAMMON   But wilt thou, Ulen,
Be constant to thy promise?
    FACE   As my life, sir.
    MAMMON   And wilt thou insinuate what I am, and praise
me,
And say I am a noble fellow?
    FACE   O, what else, sir?   340
And that you'll make her royal with the stone,
An empress; you yourself king of Bantam.

318 **by attorney** in disguise   327 **fall** veil **tire** headdress

MAMMON   Wilt thou do this?
FACE   Will I, sir!
MAMMON   Lungs, my Lungs!
I love thee.
FACE   Send your stuff, sir, that my master
May busy himself about projection.
MAMMON   Thou'st witch'd me, rogue: take, go.
                         [*Gives him money*]
FACE   Your jack, and all, sir.
MAMMON   [*hilariously*]   Thou art a villain—I will send
my jack,
350 And the weights too. Slave, I could bite thine ear.
Away, thou dost not care for me.
FACE   Not I, sir?
MAMMON   Come, I was born to make thee, my good weasel,
Set thee on a bench, and ha' thee twirl a chain
With the best lord's vermin of 'em all.
FACE   Away, sir.
MAMMON   A count, nay, a count palatine—
FACE   Good sir, go.
MAMMON   Shall not advance thee better: no, nor faster.
                         [*Exit.*]

Scene IV

[*Enter* SUBTLE *and* DOL.]

[SUBTLE]   Has he bit? has he bit?
FACE   And swallow'd, too, my Subtle.
I ha' given him line, and now he plays, i' faith.
SUBTLE   And shall we twitch him?
FACE   Thorough both the gills.
A wench is a rare bait, with which a man
No sooner's taken, but he straight firks mad.
SUBTLE   Dol, my Lord What's-hum's sister, you must **now**
Bear yourself *statelich*.
DOL COMMON   O, let me alone,
I'll not forget my race, I warrant you.
I'll keep my distance, laugh and talk aloud;
10 Have all the tricks of a proud scurvy lady,
And be as rude's her women.

347 jack a mechanical device for turning a spit 5 firks mad is stirred
up to madness

FACE   Well said, sanguine!

SUBTLE   But will he send his andirons?

FACE   His jack too,
And 's iron shoeing-horn; I ha' spoke to him. Well,
I must not lose my wary gamester yonder.

SUBTLE   O, Monsieur Caution, that will not be gull'd?

FACE   Ay,
If I can strike a fine hook into him, now!—
The Temple-church, there I have cast mine angle.
Well, pray for me. I'll about it.   *One knocks.*

SUBTLE   What, more gudgeons!   20
Dol, scout, scout!   [DOL *goes to the window.*]
                  Stay, Face, you must go to the door;
'Pray God it be my Anabaptist—Who is 't, Dol?

DOL COMMON   I know him not: he looks like a gold-end-
man.

SUBTLE   Gods so! 'tis he, he said he would send—what call
you him?
The sanctified elder, that should deal
For Mammon's jack and andirons. Let him in.
Stay, help me off, first, with my gown. [*Exit* FACE *with the*   30
gown.]   Away,
Madam, to your withdrawing chamber. Now,   [*Exit* DOL.]
In a new tune, new gesture, but old language.—
This fellow is sent from one negotiates with me
About the stone too, for the holy brethren
Of Amsterdam, the exil'd saints, that hope
To raise their discipline by it. I must use him
In some strange fashion now, to make him admire me.

SCENE V

[*Enter* ANANIAS.]

SUBTLE [*calling.*]   Where is my drudge?

[*Enter* FACE.]

FACE   Sir!

11 sanguine modern equivalent: Blondie 18 angle fish-hook 20 gudgeons small fish, *i.e.,* suckers 24 gold-end-man one who buys odds and
ends of gold 36 exiled saints a congregation of English Puritans whose
zeal had led them to migrate to Holland where the church was more
congenial to their fanaticism. Jonson uses "saints" satirically. 37 discipline Puritan form of church government

SUBTLE   Take away the recipient,
And rectify your menstrue from the phlegma.
Then pour it o' the Sol, in the cucurbite,
And let 'em macerate together.
FACE   Yes, sir.
And save the ground?
SUBTLE   No: *terra damnata*
Must not have entrance in the work.—Who are you?
ANANIAS   A faithful brother, if it please you.
SUBTLE   What's that?
A Lullianist? a Ripley? *Filius artis?*
Can you sublime and dulcify? Calcine?
10 Know you the sapor pontic? Sapor stiptic?
Or what is homogene, or heterogene?
ANANIAS   I understand no heathen language, truly.
SUBTLE   Heathen! You Knipperdoling! Is Ars sacra,
Or chrysopoeia, or spagyrica,
Or the pamphysic, or panarchic knowledge,
A heathen language?
ANANIAS   Heathen Greek, I take it.
SUBTLE   How! Heathen Greek?
ANANIAS   All's heathen but the Hebrew.
SUBTLE   Sirrah my varlet, stand you forth and speak to him
Like a philosopher; answer i' the language.
20 Name the vexations, and the martyrizations
Of metals in the work.
FACE   Sir, putrefaction,
Solution, ablution, sublimation,
Cohobation, calcination, ceration, and
Fixation.
SUBTLE   This is heathen Greek, to you, now?—
And when comes vivification?
FACE   After mortification.
SUBTLE   What's cohobation?
FACE   'Tis the pouring on
Your *aqua regis,* and then drawing him off,
To the trine circle of the seven spheres.
SUBTLE   What's the proper passion of metals?
30 FACE   Malleation.

---

7 **brother** so the Puritans called themselves. Subtle pretends to think he
means a fellow alchemist. 8 **Lullianist, Ripley** follower of Raymond
Lully or George Ripley, both famous alchemists 8 **Filius artis** son of
the art 13 **Knipperdoling** a leader of the Anabaptists

SUBTLE   What's your *ultimum supplicium auri?*

FACE   Antimonium.

SUBTLE   This's heathen Greek to you?—And what's your mercury?

FACE   A very fugitive, he will be gone, sir.

SUBTLE   How know you him?

FACE   By his viscosity,
His oleosity, and his suscitability.

SUBTLE   How do you sublime him?

FACE   With the calce of egg-shells,
White marble, talc.

SUBTLE   Your magisterium now,
What's that?

FACE   Shifting, sir, your elements,
Dry into cold, cold into moist, moist into hot,   40
Hot into dry.

SUBTLE   This's heathen Greek to you still?—
Your *lapis philosophicus?*

FACE   'Tis a stone,
And not a stone; a spirit, a soul, and a body,
Which if you do dissolve, it is dissolv'd;
If you coagulate, it is coagulated;
If you make it to fly, it flieth.

SUBTLE   Enough.   [*Exit* FACE.]
This's heathen Greek to you? What are you, sir?

ANANIAS   Please you, a servant of the exil'd brethren,
That deal with widows' and with orphans' goods,
And make a just account unto the saints: 50
A deacon.

SUBTLE   O, you are sent from Master Wholesome,
Your teacher?

ANANIAS   From Tribulation Wholesome,
Our very zealous pastor.

SUBTLE   Good! I have
Some orphans' goods to come here.

ANANIAS   Of what kind, sir?

SUBTLE   Pewter and brass, andirons and kitchen-ware;
Metals, that we must use our med'cine on:
Wherein the brethren may have a penn'orth
For ready money.

ANANIAS   Were the orphans' parents
Sincere professors?

60 professors *i.e.,* subscribers to the Puritan faith

SUBTLE   Why do you ask?

60 ANANIAS   Because
We then are to deal justly, and give, in truth,
Their utmost value.

SUBTLE   'Slid, you'd cozen else,
An if their parents were not of the faithful?—
I will not trust you, now I think on't,
Till I ha' talk'd with your pastor. Ha' you brought money
To buy more coals?

ANANIAS   No, surely.

SUBTLE   No? How so?

ANANIAS   The brethren bid me say unto you, sir,
Surely, they will not venter any more
Till they may see projection.

SUBTLE   How!

ANANIAS   You've had
70 For the instruments, as bricks, and loam, and glasses,
Already thirty pound; and for materials,
They say, some ninety more. And they have heard since,
That one at Heidelberg made it of an egg,
And a small paper of pin-dust.

SUBTLE   What's your name?

ANANIAS   My name is Ananias.

SUBTLE   Out, the varlet
That cozen'd the apostles! Hence, away!
Flee, mischief! had your holy consistory
No name to send me, of another sound
Than wicked Ananias? Send your elders
80 Hither to make atonement for you, quickly,
And gi' me satisfaction; or out goes
The fire; and down th' alembics, and the furnace,
Piger Henricus, or what not. Thou wretch!
Both *sericon* and *bufo* shall be lost,
Tell 'em. All hope of rooting out the bishops,
Or th' anti-Christian hierarchy shall perish,
If they stay threescore minutes; the aqueity,
Terreity, and sulphureity
Shall run together again, and all be annull'd,
90 Thou wicked Ananias! [*Exit* ANANIAS.] This will fetch 'em,
And make 'em haste towards their gulling more.
A man must deal like a rough nurse, and fright
Those that are froward to an appetite.

85 bishops the Puritans hated the bishops of the English church

Scene VI

[*Enter* FACE, *in his Captain's uniform, followed by*
ABEL DRUGGER.]

[FACE]   He's busy with his spirits, but we'll upon him.

SUBTLE   How now! What mates, what Bayards ha' we
here?

FACE   I told you he would be furious.—Sir, here's Nab
Has brought you another piece of gold to look on;

                            [*Aside to* DRUGGER.]

—We must appease him. Give it me,—and prays you,
You would devise—what is it, Nab?

DRUGGER   A sign, sir.

FACE   Ay, a good lucky one, a thriving sign, Doctor.

SUBTLE   I was devising now.

FACE   [*Aside to* SUBTLE.]   'Slight, do not say so,   10
He will repent he ga' you any more.—
What say you to his constellation, Doctor,
The Balance?

SUBTLE   No, that way is stale and common.
A townsman born in Taurus, gives the bull,
Or the bull's head; in Aries, the ram,—
A poor device! No, I will have his name
Form'd in some mystic character, whose *radii*,
Striking the senses of the passers-by,
Shall, by a virtual influence, breed affections,
That may result upon the party owns it: 20
As thus—

FACE   Nab!

SUBTLE   He first shall have *a bell*, that's *Abel*;
And by it standing one whose name is *Dee*,
In a *rug* gown, there's *D*, and *Rug*, that's *drug*;
And right anenst him a dog snarling *er*;
There's Drugger, Abel Drugger. That's his sign.
And here's now mystery and hieroglyphic!

FACE   Abel, thou art made.

DRUGGER   Sir, I do thank his worship.

2 **Bayards** blind horses (from the legendary horse given by Charlemagne
to the sons of Aymon. His name came to mean both "a blind horse"
and "a chivalrous person.")   14 **gives** uses as the sign for his shop
24 **Dee** Dr. John Dee, a famous astrologer (d. 1608)   25 **rug** of coarse
frieze

30   FACE   Six o' thy legs more will not do it, Nab.
He has brought you a pipe of tobacco, Doctor.
    DRUGGER   Yes, sir.
I have another thing I would impart—
    FACE   Out with it, Nab.
    DRUGGER   Sir, there is lodg'd, hard by me,
A rich young widow—
    FACE   Good! a bona roba?
    DRUGGER   But nineteen at the most.
    FACE   Very good, Abel.
    DRUGGER   Marry, she's not in fashion yet; she wears
A hood, but 't stands a cop.
    FACE   No matter, Abel.
    DRUGGER   And I do now and then give her a fucus—
    FACE   What! dost thou deal, Nab?
40   SUBTLE   I did tell you, Captain,
    DRUGGER   And physic too, sometime, sir; for which she
trusts me
With all her mind. She's come up here of purpose
To learn the fashion.
    FACE   Good (his match too!)—On, Nab.
    DRUGGER   And she does strangely long to know her fortune.
    FACE   God's lid, Nab, send her to the doctor, hither.
    DRUGGER   Yes, I have spoke to her of his worship already;
But she's afraid it will be blown abroad,
And hurt her marriage.
50   FACE   Hurt it! 'tis the way
To heal it, if 'twere hurt; to make it more
Follow'd and sought. Nab, thou shalt tell her this.
She'll be more known, more talk'd of; and your widows
Are ne'er of any price till they be famous;
Their honour is their multitude of suitors.
Send her! it may be thy good fortune. What!
Thou dost not know?
    DRUGGER   No, sir, she'll never marry
Under a knight; her brother has made a vow.
    FACE   What! and dost thou despair, my little Nab,
60 Knowing what the doctor has set down for thee,
And seeing so many o' the city dubb'd?
One glass o' thy water, with a madam I know,
Will have it done, Nab. What's her brother? a knight?

30 legs bows 34 bona roba handsome wench 38 a cop high on her head
39 fucus cosmetic 61 dubb'd knighted

DRUGGER   No, sir, a gentleman newly warm in's land, sir,
Scarce cold in his one-and-twenty, that does govern
His sister here; and is a man himself
Of some three thousand a year, and is come up
To learn to quarrel, and to live by his wits,
And will go down again, and die i' the country.

FACE   How! to quarrel?

DRUGGER   Yes, sir, to carry quarrels,   70
As gallants do; to manage 'em by line.

FACE   'Slid, Nab! The doctor is the only man
In Christendom for him. He has made a table,
With mathematical demonstrations,
Touching the art of quarrels. He will give him
An instrument to quarrel by. Go, bring 'em both,
Him and his sister. And, for thee, with her
The doctor happ'ly may persuade. Go to!
'Shalt give his worship a new damask suit
Upon the premises.

SUBTLE   O, good Captain!

FACE   He shall;   80
He is the honestest fellow, Doctor. Stay not,
No offers; bring the damask, and the parties.

DRUGGER   I'll try my power, sir.

FACE   And thy will too, Nab.

SUBTLE   'Tis good tobacco, this! What is't an ounce?

FACE   He'll send you a pound, Doctor.

SUBTLE   O no.

FACE   He will do't.
It is the goodest soul!—Abel, about it.
Thou shalt know more anon. Away, be gone.

                              [*Exit* ABEL.}

A miserable rogue, and lives with cheese,
And has the worms. That was the cause, indeed,
Why he came now: he dealt with me in private,   90
To get a med'cine for 'em.

SUBTLE   And shall, sir. This works.

FACE   A wife, a wife for one on's, my dear Subtle!
We'll e'en draw lots, and he that fails shall have
The more in goods, the other has in tail.

SUBTLE   Rather the less; for she may be so light
She may want grains.

FACE   Ay, or be such a burden,

71 by line in good form 96 grains weight

A man would scarce endure her for the whole.

SUBTLE   Faith, best let's see her first, and then determine.

FACE   Content. But Dol must ha' no breath on't.

100   SUBTLE   Mum.

Away you, to your Surly yonder, catch him.

FACE   Pray God I ha' not stay'd too long.

SUBTLE   I fear it. [*Exeunt.*]

Act III

[*Enter* PARSON TRIBULATION WHOLESOME *and*
DEACON ANANIAS.]

[TRIBULATION]   These chastisements are common to the
saints,
And such rebukes we of the separation
Must bear with willing shoulders, as the trials
Sent forth to tempt our frailties.

ANANIAS   In pure zeal,
I do not like the man; he is a heathen,
And speaks the language of Canaan, truly.

TRIBULATION   I think him a profane person indeed.

ANANIAS   He bears
The visible mark of the beast in his forehead.
And for his stone, it is a work of darkness,   10
And with philosophy blinds the eyes of man.

TRIBULATION   Good brother, we must bend unto all means
That may give furtherance to the holy cause.

ANANIAS   Which his cannot: the sanctified cause
Should have a sanctified course.

TRIBULATION .   Not always necessary.
The children of perdition are oft times
Made instruments even of the greatest works.
Besides, we should give somewhat to man's nature,
The place he lives in, still about the fire,
And fume of metals, that intoxicate   20
The brain of man, and make him prone to passion.
Where have you greater atheists than your cooks?
Or more profane, or choleric, than your glass-men?
More anti-Christian than your bell-founders?
What makes the devil so devilish, I would ask you,
Sathan, our common enemy, but his being
Perpetually about the fire, and boiling
Brimstone and arsenic? We must give, I say,
Unto the motives, and the stirrers up
Of humours in the blood. It may be so,   30
Whenas the work is done, the stone is made,

3 separation the Anabaptists, who sought refuge in Amsterdam

49

This heat of his may turn into a zeal,
And stand up for the beauteous discipline
Against the menstruous cloth and rag of Rome.
We must await his calling, and the coming
Of the good spirit. You did fault, t' upbraid him
With the brethren's blessing of Heidelberg, weighing
What need we have to hasten on the work,
For the restoring of the silenc'd saints,
40 Which ne'er will be but by the philosopher's stone.
And so a learned elder, one of Scotland,
Assur'd me; *aurum potabile* being
The only med'cine for the civil magistrate,
T' incline him to a feeling of the cause;
And must be daily us'd in the disease.
    ANANIAS   I have not edified more, truly, by man,
Not since the beautiful light first shone on me,
And I am sad my zeal hath so offended.
    TRIBULATION   Let us call on him then.
    ANANIAS   The motion's good,
50 And of the spirit; I will knock first. [*Knocks.*]
    Peace be within!

SCENE II

[SUBTLE *admits* TRIBULATION *and* ANANIAS.]

    [SUBTLE]   O, are you come? 'Twas time. Your threescore
minutes
Were at the last thread, you see; and down had gone
Furnus acediæ, turris circulatorius:
Limbec, bolt's-head, retort, and pelican
Had all been cinders. Wicked Ananias!
Art thou return'd? Nay, then, it goes down yet.
    TRIBULATION   Sir, be appeased; he is come to humble
Himself in spirit, and to ask your patience,
10 If too much zeal hath carried him aside
From the due path.
    SUBTLE   Why, this doth qualify!
    TRIBULATION   The brethren had no purpose, verily,

---

34 **menstruous** filthy, polluted 39 **silenc'd** dissenting ministers who were
not allowed to preach in English churches 42 **aurum potabile** a sovereign remedy, *i.e.,* bribery 4 **Furnus . . . circulatorius** the compound
furnace and glass still 11 **qualify** modifies the situation

To give you the least grievance; but are ready
To lend their willing hands to any project
The spirit and you direct.

  SUBTLE   This qualifies more!

  TRIBULATION And for the orphans' goods, let them be
valu'd,
Or what is needful else to the holy work,
It shall be numb'red, here, by me, the saints
Throw down their purse before you.

  SUBTLE   This qualifies most! 20
Why, thus it should be, now you understand.
Have I discours'd so unto you of our stone,
And of the good that it shall bring your cause?
Show'd you (beside the main of hiring forces
Abroad, drawing the Hollanders, your friends,
From th' Indies, to serve you, with all their fleet)
That even the med'cinal use shall make you a faction
And party in the realm? As, put the case,
That some great man in state, he have the gout,
Why, you but send three drops of your elixir, 30
You help him straight: there you have made a friend.
Another has the palsy or the dropsy,
He takes of your incombustible stuff,
He's young again: there you have made a friend.
A lady that is past the feat of body,
Though not of mind, and hath her face decay'd
Beyond all cure of paintings, you restore
With the oil of talc: there you have made a friend;
And all her friends. A lord that is a leper,
A knight that has the bone-ache, or a squire 40
That hath both these, you make 'em smooth and sound
With a bare fricace of your med'cine; still
You increase your friends.

  TRIBULATION   Ay, 'tis very pregnant.

  SUBTLE And then the turning of this lawyer's pewter
To plate at Christmas—

  ANANIAS   Christ-tide, I pray you.

  SUBTLE Yet, Ananias!

  ANANIAS   I have done.

  SUBTLE   Or changing
His parcel gilt to massy gold. You cannot

42 fricace rubbing, massage 45 Christ-tide the Puritans avoided *mass*
as a Popish word 47 parcel gilt partly gilded silverware

But raise you friends withal, to be of power
To pay an army in the field, to buy
50 The King of France out of his realms, or Spain
Out of his Indies. What can you not do
Against lords spiritual or temporal,
That shall oppone you?

TRIBULATION   Verily, 'tis true.
We may be temporal lords ourselves, I take it.

SUBTLE   You may be anything, and leave off to make
Long-winded exercises; or suck up
Your *ha!* and *hum!* in a tune. I not deny,
But such as are not graced in a state,
May, for their ends, be adverse in religion,
60 And get a tune to call the flock together.
For, to say sooth, a tune does much with women
And other phlegmatic people; it is your bell.

ANANIAS   Bells are profane; a tune may be religious.

SUBTLE   No warning with you? Then farewell my patience.
'Slight, it shall down; I will not be thus tortur'd.

TRIBULATION   I pray you, sir.

SUBTLE   All shall perish. I have spoke it.

TRIBULATION   Let me find grace, sir, in your eyes; the man,
He stands corrected: neither did his zeal,
70 But as yourself, allow a tune somewhere,
Which now, being tow'rd the stone, we shall not need.

SUBTLE   No, nor your holy vizard, to win widows
To give you legacies; or make zealous wives
To rob their husbands for the common cause;
Nor take the start of bonds broke but one day,
And say they were forfeited by providence.
Nor shall you need o'er night to eat huge meals,
To celebrate your next day's fast the better;
The whilst the brethren and the sisters humbled,
80 Abate the stiffness of the flesh. Nor cast
Before your hungry hearers scrupulous bones;
As whether a Christian may hawk or hunt,
Or whether matrons of the holy assembly
May lay their hair out, or wear doublets,
Or have that idol, starch, about their linen.

53 oppone oppose 71 tow'rd near possession of 81 scrupulous bones *i.e.,*
discussion of Puritan scruples like those given in the following lines

ANANIAS   It is indeed an idol.

TRIBULATION   Mind him not, sir.
I do command thee, spirit (of zeal, but trouble),
To peace within him! Pray you, sir, go on.

SUBTLE   Nor shall you need to libel 'gainst the prelates,
And shorten so your ears against the hearing   90
Of the next wire-drawn grace. Nor of necessity
Rail against plays, to please the alderman
Whose daily custard you devour; nor lie
With zealous rage till you are hoarse. Not one
Of these so singular arts. Nor call yourselves
By names of Tribulation, Persecution,
Restraint, Long-patience, and such like, affected
By the whole family or wood of you,
Only for glory, and to catch the ear
Of the disciple.   100

TRIBULATION   Truly, sir, they are
Ways that the godly brethren have invented,
For propagation of the glorious cause,
As very notable means, and whereby also
Themselves grow soon, and profitably, famous.

SUBTLE   O, but the stone, all's idle to't! Nothing!
The art of angels, nature's miracle,
The divine secret that doth fly in clouds
From east to west, and whose tradition
Is not from men, but spirits.

ANANIAS   I hate traditions;   110
I do not trust them—

TRIBULATION   Peace!

ANANIAS   They are popish all.
I will not peace! I will not—

TRIBULATION   Ananias!

ANANIAS   Please the profane, to grieve the godly!
     I may not.

SUBTLE   Well, Ananias, thou shalt overcome.

TRIBULATION   It is an ignorant zeal that haunts him, sir,
But truly else a very faithful brother,
A botcher, and a man by revelation
That hath a competent knowledge of the truth.

SUBTLE   Has he a competent sum there i' the bag   120
To buy the goods within? I am made guardian,

90 shorten have them cut off in the pillory as punishment 98 **wood**
assemblage 118 **botcher** mender, petty tailor

And must, for charity and conscience' sake,
Now see the most be made for my poor orphan,
Though I desire the brethren, too, good gainers;
There they are within. When you have view'd and bought
'em,
And ta'en the inventory of what they are,
They are ready for projection; there's no more
To do: cast on the med'cine, so much silver

130 As there is tin there, so much gold as brass,
I'll gi' it you in by weight.

    TRIBULATION   But how long time,
Sir, must the saints expect yet?

    SUBTLE   Let me see,
How's the moon now? Eight, nine, ten days hence,
He will be silver potate; then three days
Before he citronize. Some fifteen days,
The magisterium will be perfected.

    ANANIAS   About the second day of the third week,
In the ninth month?

    SUBTLE   Yes, my good Ananias.

    TRIBULATION   What will the orphans' goods arise to, think

140 you?

    SUBTLE   Some hundred marks, as much as fill'd three cars,
Unladed now: you'll make six millions of 'em—
But I must ha' more coals laid in.

    TRIBULATION   How?

    SUBTLE   Another load,
And then we ha' finish'd. We must now increase
Our fire to *ignis ardens;* we are past
Fimus equinus, balnei, cineris,
And all those lenter heats. If the holy purse
Should with this draught fall low, and that the saints
Do need a present sum, I have a trick

150 To melt the pewter, you shall buy now instantly,
And with a tincture make you as good Dutch dollars
As any are in Holland.

    TRIBULATION   Can you so?

    SUBTLE   Ay, and shall bide the third examination.

    ANANIAS   It will be joyful tidings to the brethren.

    SUBTLE   But you must carry it secret.

    TRIBULATION   Ay; but stay,

135 citronize turn yellow 146 Fimus . . . cineris Three gradations of
heat: from horse-dung, hot water, ashes

This act of coining, is it lawful?

ANANIAS   Lawful!
We know no magistrate; or, if we did,
This's foreign coin.

SUBTLE   It is no coining, sir.
It is but casting.

TRIBULATION   Ha! you distinguish well;   160
Casting of money may be lawful.

ANANIAS   'Tis, sir.

TRIBULATION   Truly, I take it so.

SUBTLE   There is no scruple,
Sir, to be made of it; believe Ananias;
This case of conscience he is studied in.

TRIBULATION   I'll make a question of it to the brethren.

ANANIAS   The brethren shall approve it lawful, doubt not.
Where shall't be done?

SUBTLE   For that we'll talk anon.
                              Knock without.
There's some to speak with me. Go in, I pray you,
And view the parcels. That's the inventory.   170
I'll come to you straight. [*Exeunt* TRIBULATION *and* ANANIAS.]
    Who is it?—Face! appear.

SCENE III

[*Enter* FACE *in his captain's uniform.*]

[SUBTLE]   How now! good prize?

FACE   Good pox! Yond' costive cheater
Never came on.

SUBTLE   How then?

FACE   I ha' walk'd the round
Till now, and no such thing.

SUBTLE   And ha' you quit him?

FACE   Quit him! An hell would quit him too, he were
happy.
'Slight! would you have me stalk like a mill-jade,
All day, for one that will not yield us grains?
I know him of old.

SUBTLE   O, but to ha' gull'd him,
Had been a mastery.

1 cheater Surly

FACE   Let him go, black boy!
10 And turn thee, that some fresh news may possess thee.
A noble count, a don of Spain (my dear
Delicious compeer, and my party-bawd),
Who is come hither private for his conscience
And brought munition with him, six great slops,
Bigger than three Dutch hoys, beside round trunks,
Furnish'd with pistolets, and pieces of eight,
Will straight be here, my rogue, to have thy bath,
(That is the colour) and to make his batt'ry
Upon our Dol, our castle, our cinqueport,
20 Our Dover pier, our what thou wilt. Where is she?
She must prepare perfumes, delicate linen,
The bath in chief, a banquet, and her wit,
For she must milk his epididymis.
Where is the doxy?
SUBTLE   I'll send her to thee;
And but despatch my brace of little John Leydens
And come again myself.
FACE   Are they within then?
SUBTLE   Numb'ring the sum.
FACE   How much?
SUBTLE   A hundred marks, boy. [*Exit.*]
FACE   Why, this's a lucky day. Ten pounds of Mammon!
Three o' my clerk! A portague o' my grocer!
30 This o' the brethren! Beside reversions
And states to come, i' the widow, and my count!
My share to-day will not be bought for forty—

[*Enter* DOL.]

DOL COMMON   What?
FACE   Pounds, dainty Dorothy! Art thou so near?
DOL COMMON   Yes. Say, lord general, how fares our camp?
FACE   As with the few that had entrench'd themselves
Safe, by their discipline, against a world, Dol,
And laugh'd within those trenches, and grew fat
With thinking on the booties, Dol, brought in
Daily by their small parties. This dear hour,
40 A doughty don is taken with my Dol;

12 **party** partner 14 **slops** padded breeches 15 **hoys** small sloops
15 **trunks** hose 16 **pistolets** Spanish gold coins worth about three to four
dollars **pieces of eight** coins 18 **colour** pretext 19 **cinqueport, Dover
pier** English ports of entry on the Channel 24 **doxy** whore 25 **John
Leydens** Puritans

And thou mayst make his ransom what thou wilt,
My Dowsabel; he shall be brought here, fetter'd
With thy fair looks, before he sees thee; and thrown
In a down-bed, as dark as any dungeon;
Where thou shalt keep him waking with thy drum;
Thy drum, my Dol, thy drum; till he be tame
As the poor blackbirds were i' the great frost,
Or bees are with a basin; and so hive him
I' the swan-skin coverlid and cambric sheets,
Till he work honey and wax, my little God's-gift.   5c

   DOL COMMON   What is he, General?
   FACE   An *adalantado*,
A grandee, girl. Was not my Dapper here yet?
   DOL COMMON   No.
   FACE   Nor my Drugger?
   DOL COMMON   Neither.
   FACE   A pox on 'em,
They are so long a furnishing! such stinkards
Would not be seen upon these festival days.—

                 [*Re-enter* SUBTLE.]

How now! ha' you done?
   SUBTLE   Done. They are gone; the sum
Is here in bank, my Face. I would we knew
Another chapman now would buy 'em outright.
   FACE   'Slid, Nab shall do't against he ha' the widow,   60
To furnish household.
   SUBTLE   Excellent, well thought on.
Pray God he come.
   FACE   I pray he keep away
Till our new business be o'erpast.
   SUBTLE   But, Face,
How cam'st thou by this secret don?
   FACE   A spirit
Brought me th' intelligence in a paper here,
As I was conjuring yonder in my circle
For Surly; I ha' my flies abroad. Your bath
Is famous, Subtle, by my means. Sweet Dol,
You must go tune your virginal, no losing
O' the least time. And—do you hear?—good action!   7a

---

42 **Dowsabel** English form of name Dulcibella 47 **great frost** of 1608
50 **God's-gift** Greek meaning of Dorothea 51 **adalantado** a Spanish governor (of a province) 69 **virginal** spinet

Firk like a flounder; kiss like a scallop, close;
And tickle him with thy mother-tongue. His great
Verdugoship has not a jot of language;
So much the easier to be cozen'd, my Dolly.
He will come here in a hir'd coach, obscure,
And our own coachman, whom I have sent as guide,
No creature else.—Who's that?
                One knocks. [DOL *goes to the window.*]
    SUBTLE   It is not he?
    FACE   O no, not yet this hour.
    SUBTLE   Who is't?
    DOL COMMON   Dapper,
Your clerk.
    FACE   God's will then, Queen of Faery,
80 On with your tire; [*Exit* DOL.] and, Doctor, with your robes.
Let's despatch him for God's sake.
    SUBTLE   'Twill be long.
    FACE   I warrant you, take but the cues I give you,
It shall be brief enough.   [*Goes to the window.*]
      'Slight, here are more!
Abel, and, I think, the angry boy, the heir,
That fain would quarrel.
    SUBTLE   And the widow?
    FACE   No,
Not that I see. Away!   [*Exit* SUBTLE.]

Scene IV

[FACE *admits* DAPPER.]

   [FACE]   O, sir, you are welcome.
The doctor is within a-moving for you.—
I have had the most ado to win him to it!—
He swears you'll be the darling o' the dice;
He never heard her Highness dote till now, he says.
Your aunt has giv'n you the most gracious words
That can be thought on.
    DAPPER   Shall I see her Grace?
    FACE   See her, and kiss her too.—

71 Firk move briskly 73 Verdugoship The Spanish word means "exe-
cutioner" language *i.e.,* English 80 tire attire, costume

[*Enter* ABEL DRUGGER, *followed by* KASTRIL.]

                          What, honest Nab!

Hast brought the damask?

    DRUGGER   No, sir; here's tobacco.

    FACE   'Tis well done, Nab; thou'lt bring the damask too?

    DRUGGER   Yes. Here's the gentleman, Captain, Master   10
Kastril,

I have brought to see the doctor.

    FACE   Where's the widow?

    DRUGGER   Sir, as he likes, his sister, he says, shall come.

    FACE   O, is it so? Good time. Is your name Kastril, sir?

    KASTRIL   Ay, and the best o' the Kastrils, I'd be sorry else,

By fifteen hundred a year. Where is this doctor?

My mad tobacco-boy here tells me of one

That can do things. Has he any skill?

    FACE   Wherein, sir?

    KASTRIL   To carry a business, manage a quarrel fairly,

Upon fit terms.

    FACE   It seems, sir, y' are but young   20

About the town, that can make that a question.

    KASTRIL   Sir, not so young but I have heard some speech

Of the angry boys, and seen 'em take tobacco;

And in his shop; and I can take it too.

And I would fain be one of 'em, and go down

And practise i' the country.

    FACE   Sir, for the duello,

The doctor, I assure you, shall inform you,

To the least shadow of a hair; and show you

An instrument he has of his own making,

Wherewith, no sooner shall you make report   30

Of any quarrel, but he will take the height on't

Most instantly, and tell in what degree

Of safety it lies in, or mortality.

And how it may be borne, whether in a right line,

Or a half circle; or may else be cast

Into an angle blunt, if not acute:

All this he will demonstrate. And then, rules

To give and take the lie by.

    KASTRIL   How! to take it?

    FACE   Yes, in oblique he'll show you, or in circle;

But never in diameter. The whole town   40

23 **angry boys** riotous youths, sports   39 **oblique, circle** the lie circum-
stantial   40 **diameter** the lie direct

Study his theorems, and dispute them ordinarily
At the eating academies.

KASTRIL   But does he teach
Living by the wits too?

FACE   Anything whatever.
You cannot think that subtlety but he reads it.
He made me a captain. I was a stark pimp,
Just o' your standing, 'fore I met with him;
It's not two months since. I'll tell you his method:
First, he will enter you at some ordinary.

KASTRIL   No, I'll not come there; you shall pardon me.

50 FACE   For why, sir?

KASTRIL   There's gaming there, and tricks.

FACE   Why, would you be
A gallant, and not game?

KASTRIL   Ay, 'twill spend a man.

FACE   Spend you! It will repair you when you are spent.
How do they live by their wits there, that have vented
Six times your fortunes?

KASTRIL   What, three thousand a year!

FACE   Ay, forty thousand.

KASTRIL   Are there such?

FACE   Ay, sir,
And gallants yet. Here's a young gentleman
Is born to nothing,—[*points to* DAPPER.] forty
    marks a year,
Which I count nothing—he's to be initiated,
60 And have a fly o' the doctor. He will win you
By unresistible luck, within this fortnight,
Enough to buy a barony. They will set him
Upmost, at the groom porter's, all the Christmas;
And for the whole year through at every place
Where there is play, present him with the chair,
The best attendance, the best drink, sometimes
Two glasses of Canary, and pay nothing;
The purest linen and the sharpest knife,
The partridge next his trencher, and somewhere
70 The dainty bed, in private, with the dainty.
You shall ha' your ordinaries bid for him,
As playhouses for a poet; and the master

48 **ordinary** restaurant 54 **,vented** spent 63 **groom porter** an officer of
the royal household in charge of gaming. He provided materials, set-
tled disputes, and had the privilege of keeping a free table at Christmas

Pray him aloud to name what dish he affects,
Which must be butter'd shrimps; and those that drink
To no mouth else, will drink to his, as being
The goodly president mouth of all the board.

    KASTRIL   Do you not gull one?

    FACE   'Ods my life! Do you think it?
You shall have a cast commander, (can but get
In credit with a glover, or a spurrier,
For some two pair of either's ware aforehand)   80
Will, by most swift posts, dealing with him,
Arrive at competent means to keep himself,
His punk, and naked boy, in excellent fashion,
And be admir'd for 't.

    KASTRIL   Will the doctor teach this?

    FACE   He will do more, sir. When your land is gone,
(As men of spirit hate to keep earth long),
In a vacation, when small money is stirring,
And ordinaries suspended till the term,
He'll show a perspective, where on one side
You shall behold the faces and the persons   90
Of all sufficient young heirs in town,
Whose bonds are current for commodity;
On th' other side, the merchants' forms, and others,
That without help of any second broker,
Who would expect a share, will trust such parcels;
In the third square, the very street and sign
Where the commodity dwells, and does but wait
To be deliver'd, be it pepper, soap,
Hops, or tobacco, oatmeal, woad, or cheeses.
All which you may so handle, to enjoy   100
To your own use, and never stand oblig'd.

    KASTRIL   I' faith! is he such a fellow?

    FACE   Why, Nab here knows him.
And then for making matches for rich widows,
Young gentlewomen, heirs, the fortunat'st man!
He's sent to, far and near, all over England,
To have his counsel, and to know their fortunes.

    KASTRIL   God's will, my suster shall see him.

78 cast cashiered   87 vacation *i.e.,* when the law courts are not sitting
89 perspective an ingeniously made picture; the appearance of which
changes with the spectator's point of view or which looks distorted unless seen from a certain angle. Another form could be properly seen only
through a small hole in a piece of paper   92 commodity cf. p. 22 l. 14
99 woad a dyestuff

FACE   I'll tell you, sir,
What he did tell me of Nab. It's a strange thing—
(By the way, you must eat no cheese, Nab, it breeds mel-
110 ancholy,
And that same melancholy breeds worms) but pass it—
He told me honest Nab here was ne'er at tavern
But once in's life.
    DRUGGER   Truth, and no more I was not.
    FACE   And then he was so sick—
    DRUGGER   Could he tell you that too?
    FACE   How should I know it?
    DRUGGER   In troth, we had been a-shooting,
And had a piece of fat ram-mutton to supper,
That lay so heavy o' my stomach—
    FACE   And he has no head
To bear any wine; for what with the noise o' the fiddlers,
And care of his shop, for he dares keep no servants—
120   DRUGGER   My head did so ache—
    FACE   As he was fain to be brought home.
The doctor told me. And then a good old woman—
    DRUGGER   Yes, faith, she dwells in Seacoal-lane,—did cure
me,
With sodden ale, and pellitory o' the wall;
Cost me but twopence. I had another sickness
Was worse than that.
    FACE   Ay, that was with the grief
Thou took'st for being 'cess'd at eighteenpence
For the waterwork.
    DRUGGER   In truth, and it was like
T' have cost me almost my life.
130   FACE   Thy hair went off?
    DRUGGER   Yes, sir; 'twas done for spite.
    FACE   Nay, so says the doctor.
    KASTRIL   Pray thee, tobacco-boy, go fetch my suster;
I'll see this learned boy before I go;
And so shall she.
    FACE   Sir, he is busy now,
But if you have a sister to fetch hither,
Perhaps your own pains may command her sooner;
And he by that time will be free.
    KASTRIL   I go.   [*Exit.*]
    FACE   Drugger, she's thine! The damask!   [*Exit* ABEL.]
125 **pellitory** an herb   128 **'cess'd** assessed, taxed

[*Aside.*] Subtle and I
Must wrastle for her.—Come on, Master Dapper,
You see how I turn clients here away, **140**
To give your cause dispatch. Ha' you perform'd
The ceremonies were enjoin'd you?

DAPPER Yes, o' the vinegar,
And the clean shirt.

FACE 'Tis well; that shirt may do you
More worship than you think. Your aunt's afire,
But that she will not show it, t' have a sight on you.
Ha' you provided for her Grace's servants?

DAPPER Yes, here are six score Edward shillings.

FACE Good!

DAPPER And an old Harry's sovereign.

FACE Very good!

DAPPER And three James shillings, and an Elizabeth groat,
Just twenty nobles.

FACE O, you are too just. **150**
I would you had had the other noble in Maries.

DAPPER I have some Philip and Maries.

FACE Ay, those same
Are best of all; where are they? Hark, the doctor.

SCENE V

[*Enter* SUBTLE, *dressed like a priest of Faery and carrying
a robe for* DRUGGER *and a blindfold.*]

[SUBTLE, *in a disguised voice.*] Is yet her Grace's cousin
come?

FACE He is come.

SUBTLE And is he fasting?

FACE Yes.

SUBTLE And hath cried "hum"?

FACE Thrice, you must answer.

DAPPER Thrice.

SUBTLE And as oft "buz"?

FACE If you have, say.

DAPPER I have.

147 **Edward shillings** coined in the reign of Edward VI 151 **Maries**
coins of the reign of Queen Mary. Some bore her head and that of
Philip II, her consort.

SUBTLE   Then, to her cuz,
Hoping that he hath vinegar'd his senses,
As he was bid, the Faery Queen dispenses,
By me, this robe, the petticoat of Fortune;
Which that he straight put on, she doth importune.
And though to Fortune near be her petticoat,
10 Yet nearer is her smock, the Queen doth note,
And therefore, even of that a piece she hath sent,
Which, being a child, to wrap him in was rent;
And prays him for a scarf he now will wear it,
With as much love as then her Grace did tear it,
About his eyes, to show he is fortunate;

They [blindfold] him with a rag.

And, trusting unto her to make his state,
He'll throw away all worldly pelf about him;
Which that he will perform, she doth not doubt him.
FACE   She need not doubt him, sir. Alas, he has nothing
20 But what he will part withal as willingly,
Upon her Grace's word—throw away your purse—
As she would ask it—handkerchiefs and all—
She cannot bid that thing but he'll obey.—
If you have a ring about you, cast it off,
Or a silver seal at your wrist; her Grace will send

He throws away, as they bid him.

Her fairies here to search you, therefore deal
Directly with her Highness. If they find
That you conceal a mite, you are undone.
DAPPER   Truly, there's all.
FACE   All what?
DAPPER   My money; truly.
30 FACE   Keep nothing that is transitory about you.
[*Aside to* SUBTLE.]   Bid Dol play music.—Look, the
elves are come

DOL enters with a cittern.

To pinch you, if you tell not truth. Advise you.

They pinch him.

DAPPER   O! I have a paper with a spur-ryal in't.
FACE   *Ti, ti.*
They knew't, they say.
SUBTLE   *Ti, ti, ti, ti.* He has more yet.
FACE   *Ti, ti-ti-ti.* I' the tother pocket?

27 **Directly** straightforwardly 31 **cittern** a stringed instrument somewhat
like a modern guitar 33 **spur-ryal** a gold coin of Edward IV

SUBTLE   *Titi, titi, titi, titi.*
They must pinch him or he will never confess, they say.
                          [*They pinch him again.*]
  DAPPER   O, O!
  FACE   Nay, pray you, hold; he is her Grace's nephew!
Ti, ti, ti? What care you? Good faith, you shall care.—   40
Deal plainly, sir, and shame the fairies. Show
You are an innocent.
  DAPPER   By this good light, I ha' nothing.
  SUBTLE   *Ti ti, ti ti to ta.* He does equivocate, she says:
Ti, ti do ti, ti ti do, ti da; and swears by the light when he is
blinded.
  DAPPER   By this good dark, I ha' nothing but a half-crown
Of gold about my wrist, that my love gave me;
And a leaden heart I wore sin' she forsook me.
  FACE   I thought 'twas something. And would you incur
Your aunt's displeasure for these trifles? Come,   50
I had rather you had thrown away twenty half-crowns.
                                      [*Takes it off.*]
You may wear your leaden heart still.—[*Aside to* DOL, *who
    has come from the window.*] How now!
  SUBTLE [*Aside.*]   What news, Dol?
  DOL COMMON [*Aside.*]   Yonder's your knight, Sir Mam-
mon.
  FACE [*Aside.*]   God's lid, we never thought of him till
now!
Where is he?
  DOL COMMON [*Aside.*]   Here, hard by. He's at the door.
  SUBTLE [*Aside.*]   And you are not ready now! Dol, get   60
his suit.   [*Exit* DOL.]
He must not be sent back.
  FACE [*Aside.*]   O, by no means.
What shall we do with this same puffin here,
Now he's o' the spit?
  SUBTLE [*Aside.*]   Why, lay him back awhile,
With some device.
           [*Re-enter* DOL *with* FACE's *clothes.*]
                —*Ti, ti ti, ti ti ti.* Would her Grace speak
      with me?
I come.—[*Aside.*]   Help, Dol!

61 **his suit** *i.e.,* Face's laboratory assistant's clothes 64 **puffin** a sea-bird
(term of derision) 68 **Help, Dol!** *i.e.,* Face wants Dol to help him get
out of his uniform and into his laboratory assistant's clothes to receive
Mammon.

FACE   —Who's there? Sir Epicure,
He speaks through the keyhole, the other
knocking.

My master's i' the way. Please you to walk
70 Three or four turns, but till his back be turn'd,
And I am for you.—[*Aside.*]   Quickly, Dol!
SUBTLE   Her Grace
Commends her kindly to you, Master Dapper.

DAPPER   I long to see her Grace.

SUBTLE   She now is set
At dinner in her bed, and she has sent you
From her own private trencher, a dead mouse
And a piece of gingerbread, to be merry withal
And stay your stomach, lest you faint with fasting.
Yet if you could hold out till she saw you, she says,
It would be better for you.

FACE   Sir, he shall
80 Hold out, an't were this two hours, for her Highness;
I can assure you that. We will not lose
All we ha' done.—

SUBTLE   He must nor see, nor speak
To anybody, till then.

FACE   For that we'll put, sir,
A stay in's mouth.

SUBTLE   Of what?

FACE   Of gingerbread.
Make you it fit. He that hath pleas'd her Grace
Thus far, shall not now crinkle for a little.—
Gape, sir, and let him fit you.

[*They thrust a gag of gingerbread into his mouth.*]
SUBTLE [*Aside.*]   —Where shall we now
Bestow him?

DOL COMMON [*Aside.*]   I' the privy.—

90 SUBTLE   Come along, sir,
I now must show you Fortune's privy lodgings.

FACE   Are they perfum'd, and his bath ready?

SUBTLE   All;
Only the fumigation's somewhat strong.

FACE [*Speaking through the keyhole.*]   Sir Epicure, I am
yours, sir, by and by.   [*Exeunt with* DAPPER.]

86 **crinkle** turn aside from his purpose

Act IV

[FACE, *dressed as a laboratory assistant, admits*
MAMMON.]

[FACE] O, sir, y' are come i' the only finest time.—
MAMMON Where's Master?
FACE   Now preparing for projection, **sir**.
Your stuff will be all chang'd shortly.
MAMMON   Into gold?
FACE To gold and silver, sir.
MAMMON   Silver I care not for.
FACE Yes, sir, a little to give beggars.
MAMMON   Where's the lady?
FACE At hand here. I ha' told her such brave things
    o' you,
Touching your bounty and your noble spirit—
MAMMON   Hast thou?
FACE As she is almost in her fit to see you.
But, good sir, no divinity i' your conference,
For fear of putting her in rage.
MAMMON   I warrant thee.   10
FACE Six men will not hold her down. And then,
If the old man should hear or see you—
MAMMON   Fear not.
FACE The very house, sir, would run mad. You know **it**,
How scrupulous he is, and violent,
'Gainst the least act of sin. Physic or mathematics,
Poetry, state, or bawdry, as I told you,
She will endure, and never startle; but
No word of controversy.
MAMMON   I am school'd, good *Ulen*.
FACE And you must praise her house, remember **that**,
And her nobility.
MAMMON   Let me alone: 20
No herald, no, nor antiquary, Lungs,
Shall do it better. Go.
FACE [*Aside.*] Why, this is yet
A kind of modern happiness, to have

16 **state** politics 23 **happiness** appropriateness
67

Dol Common for a great lady.   *[Exit.]*

MAMMON   Now, Epicure,
Heighten thyself, talk to her all in gold;
Rain her as many showers as Jove did drops
Unto his Danaë; show the god a miser,
Compar'd with Mammon. What! the stone will do't.
She shall feel gold, taste gold, hear gold, sleep gold;
30 Nay, we will *concumbere* gold. I will be puissant
And mighty in my talk to her.—

    [Re-enter FACE *with* DOL *richly dressed.]*

    Here she comes.
FACE [*Aside.*]   To him, Dol, suckle him.—This is
    the noble knight
I told your ladyship—
MAMMON   Madam, with your pardon,
I kiss your vesture.
DOL COMMON   Sir, I were uncivil
If I would suffer that; my lip to you, sir.
MAMMON   I hope my lord your brother be in health, lady.
DOL COMMON   My lord my brother is, though I no lady, sir.
FACE [*Aside.*]   Well said, my Guinea bird.
MAMMON   Right noble madam—
FACE [*Aside.*]   O, we shall have most fierce idolatry.
MAMMON   'Tis your prerogative.
40 DOL COMMON   Rather your courtesy.
MAMMON   Were there nought else t' enlarge your virtues
to me,
These answers speak your breeding and your blood.
DOL COMMON   Blood we boast none, sir; a poor baron's
daughter.
MAMMON   Poor! and gat you? Profane not. Had your
father
Slept all the happy remnant of his life
After the act, lien but there still, and panted,
50 He'd done enough to make himself, his issue,
And his posterity noble.
DOL COMMON   Sir, although
We may be said to want the gilt and trappings,
The dress of honour, yet we strive to keep
The seeds and the materials.
MAMMON   I do see

30 **concumbere** fornicate 38 **Guinea bird** slang for prostitute

The old ingredient, virtue, was not lost,
Nor the drug, money, us'd to make your compound.
There is a strange nobility i' your eye,
This lip, that chin! Methinks you do resemble
One o' the Austriac princes.

    FACE [*Aside.*]   Very like! 60
Her father was an Irish costermonger.

    MAMMON   The house of Valois, just, had such a nose,
And such a forehead yet the Medici
Of Florence boast.

    DOL COMMON   Troth, and I have been lik'ned
To all these princes.

    FACE [*Aside.*]   I'll be sworn, I heard it.

    MAMMON   I know not how! it is not any one,
But e'en the very choice of all their features.

    FACE [*Aside.*]   I'll in, and laugh.   [*Exit.*]

    MAMMON   A certain touch, or air,
That sparkles a divinity beyond
An earthly beauty!

    DOL COMMON   O, you play the courtier.

    MAMMON   Good lady, gi' me leave—

    DOL COMMON   In faith, I may not, 70
To mock me, sir.

    MAMMON   To burn i' this sweet flame;
The phœnix never knew a nobler death.

    DOL COMMON   Nay, now you court the courtier, and destroy
What you would build. This art, sir, i' your words,
Calls your whole faith in question.

    MAMMON   By my soul—

    DOL COMMON   Nay, oaths are made o' the same air, sir.

    MAMMON   Nature
Never bestow'd upon mortality
A more unblam'd, a more harmonious feature;
She play'd the step-dame in all faces else.
Sweet madam, le' me be particular— 80

    DOL COMMON   Particular, sir! I pray you, know your distance.

    MAMMON   In no ill sense, sweet lady, but to ask
How your fair graces pass the hours? I see
Y' are lodg'd here, i' the house of a rare man,
An excellent artist; but what's that to you?

    DOL COMMON   Yes, sir. I study here the mathematics,

80 particular familiar 87 mathematics astrology

And distillation.

MAMMON   O, I cry your pardon.
He's a divine instructor! can extract
90 The souls of all things by his art; call all
The virtues and the miracles of the sun
Into a temperate furnace; teach dull nature
What her own forces are. A man, the emp'ror
Has courted above Kelley; sent his medals
And chains t' invite him.

DOL COMMON   Ay, and for his physic, sir—
MAMMON   Above the art of Æsculapius,
That drew the envy of the thunderer!
I know all this, and more.

DOL COMMON   Troth, I am taken, sir,
Whole with these studies that contemplate nature.
100 MAMMON   It is a noble humour; but this form
Was not intended to so dark a use.
Had you been crooked, foul, of some coarse mould,
A cloister had done well; but such a feature,
That might stand up the glory of a kingdom,
To live recluse is a mere solecism,
Though in a nunnery. It must not be.
I muse, my lord your brother will permit it!
You should spend half my land first, were I he.
Does not this diamond better on my finger
Than i' the quarry?

DOL COMMON   Yes.
110 MAMMON   Why, you are like it.
You were created, lady, for the light.
Here, you shall wear it; take it, the first pledge
Of what I speak, to bind you to believe me.

DOL COMMON   In chains of adamant?
MAMMON   Yes, the strongest bands.
And take a secret too.—Here, by your side,
Doth stand this hour the happiest man in Europe.

DOL COMMON   You are contented, sir?
MAMMON   Nay, in true being,
The envy of princes and the fear of states.

DOL COMMON   Say you so, Sir Epicure?
120 MAMMON   Yes, and thou shalt prove it,

88 **distillation** chemistry 94 **Kelley** (d. 1595) an alchemist, associate of
Dr. Dee. Rudolph II of Germany was one of his dupes 97 **thunderer**
Zeus, who killed the physician Æsculapius with a thunderbolt

Daughter of honour. I have cast mine eye
Upon thy form, and I will rear this beauty
Above all styles.

    DOL COMMON   You mean no treason, sir?

    MAMMON   No, I will take away that jealousy.
I am the lord of the philosopher's stone,
And thou the lady.

    DOL COMMON   How, sir! ha' you that?

    MAMMON   I am the master of the mastery.
This day the good old wretch here o' the house
Has made it for us. Now he's at projection.   130
Think therefore thy first wish now, let me hear it;
And it shall rain into thy lap, no shower,
But floods of gold, whole cataracts, a deluge,
To get a nation on thee.

    DOL COMMON   You are pleas'd, sir,
To work on the ambition of our sex.

    MAMMON   I'm pleas'd the glory of her sex should know,
This nook here of the Friars is no climate
For her to live obscurely in, to learn
Physic and surgery, for the constable's wife
Of some odd hundred in Essex; but come forth,   140
And taste the air of palaces; eat, drink
The toils of emp'rics, and their boasted practice;
Tincture of pearl, and coral, gold, and amber;
Be seen at feasts and triumphs; have it ask'd,
What miracle she is; set all the eyes
Of court a-fire, like a burning glass,
And work 'em into cinders, when the jewels
Of twenty states adorn thee, and the light
Strikes out the stars; that, when thy name is mention'd,
Queens may look pale; and, we but showing our love,   150
Nero's Poppæa may be lost in story!
Thus will we have it.

    DOL COMMON   I could well consent, sir.
But in a monarchy, how will this be?
The prince will soon take notice, and both seize
You and your stone, it being a wealth unfit

---

128 **mastery** art of transmutation, magisterium   137 **Friars** Blackfriars
district of London, in which Lovewit's house is located and which also
contained the theatre in which the play was probably first performed
140 **hundred** subdivision of a county   142 **emp'rics** laboratory scientists,
alchemists

For any private subject.

    MAMMON   If he knew it.

    DOL COMMON   Yourself do boast it, sir.

    MAMMON   To thee, my life.

    DOL COMMON   O, but beware, sir! you may come to end
The remnant of your days in a loath'd prison,
By speaking of it.

160   MAMMON   'Tis no idle fear!
We'll therefore go with all, my girl, and live
In a free state, where we will eat our mullets,
Sous'd in high-country wines, sup pheasants' eggs,
And have our cockles boil'd in silver shells;
Our shrimps to swim again, as when they liv'd,
In a rare butter made of dolphins' milk,
Whose cream does look like opals; and with these
Delicate meats set ourselves high for pleasure,
And take us down again, and then renew
170 Our youth and strength with drinking the elixir;
And so enjoy a perpetuity
Of life and lust! And thou shalt ha' thy wardrobe
Richer than Nature's, still to change thyself,
And vary oft'ner for thy pride than she,
Or Art, her wise and almost-equal servant.

                [Re-enter FACE.]

    FACE   Sir, you are too loud. I hear you every word
Into the laboratory. Some fitter place;
The garden, or great chamber above. *[Aside.]* How like you
her?

180   MAMMON   Excellent, Lungs! There's for thee.

                [Gives him money.]

    FACE   But do you hear?
Good sir, beware, no mention of the rabbins.

    MAMMON   We think not on 'em.

    FACE   O, it is well, sir. *[Exeunt MAMMON and DOL.]*
                    —Subtle!

SCENE II

            [Enter SUBTLE.]

Dost thou not laugh?

    SUBTLE   Yes; are they gone?

    FACE   All's clear.

SUBTLE   The widow is come.

FACE   And your quarreling disciple?

SUBTLE   Ay.

FACE   I must to my captainship again then.

SUBTLE   Stay, bring 'em in first.

FACE   So I meant. What is she?
A bonnibel?

SUBTLE   I know not.

FACE   We'll draw lots;
You'll stand to that?

SUBTLE   What else?

FACE   O, for a suit,
To fall now like a curtain, flap!

SUBTLE   To th' door, man.

FACE   You'll ha' the first kiss, 'cause I am not ready.
                                        [*Exit.*]

SUBTLE   Yes, and perhaps hit you through both the nostrils.   10

FACE [*Within.*]   Who would you speak with?

KASTRIL [*Within.*]   Where's the Captain?

FACE [*Within.*]   Gone, sir,
About some business.

KASTRIL [*Within.*]   Gone!

FACE [*Within.*]   He'll return straight.
But Master Doctor, his lieutenant, is here.

[*Enter* KASTRIL, *followed by* DAME PLIANT.]

SUBTLE   Come near, my worshipful boy, my *terræ fili*,
That is, my boy of land; make thy approaches.
Welcome; I know thy lusts and thy desires,
And I will serve and satisfy 'em. Begin,
Charge me from thence, or thence, or in this line;
Here is my centre: ground thy quarrel.

KASTRIL   You lie.   20

SUBTLE   How, child of wrath and anger! the loud lie?
For what, my sudden boy?

KASTRIL   Nay, that look you to,
I am aforehand.

SUBTLE   O, this's no true grammar,

4 captainship *i.e.,* go and put on his captain's uniform again   6 **bonnibel**
pretty girl   8 **To fall . . . flap!** *i.e.,* so that he could change his suit without leaving Subtle alone with the girl   10 **hit . . . nostrils** put your nose
out of joint

And as ill logic! You must render causes, child,
Your first and second intentions, know your canons
And your divisions, moods, degrees, and differences,
Your predicaments, substance, and accident,
Series extern and intern, with their causes
Efficient, material, formal, final,
And ha' your elements perfect—

30   KASTRIL   What is this?
The angry tongue he talks in?
    SUBTLE   That false precept,
Of being aforehand, has deceiv'd a number,
And made 'em enter quarrels oftentimes
Before they were aware; and afterward,
Against their wills.
    KASTRIL   How must I do then, sir?
    SUBTLE   I cry this lady mercy; she should first
Have been saluted. I do call you lady,
Because you are to be one ere't be long,
My soft and buxom widow.   *He kisses her.*
    KASTRIL   Is she, i' faith?
40   SUBTLE   Yes, or my art is an egregious liar.
    KASTRIL   How know you?
    SUBTLE   By inspection on her forehead,
And subtlety of her lip, which must be tasted
Often to make a judgment.   *He kisses her again.*
               'Slight, she melts
Like a myrobolane. Here is yet a line,
In *rivo frontis,* tells me he is no knight.
    DAME PLIANT   What is he then, sir?
    SUBTLE   Let me see your hand.
O, your *linea fortunæ* makes it plain;
And *stella* here *in monte veneris.*
But, most of all, *junctura annularis.*
50 He is a soldier, or a man of art, lady,
But shall have some great honour shortly.
    DAME PLIANT   Brother,
He's a rare man, believe me!
        [*Re-enter* FACE, *in his uniform.*]

24 **render causes** Subtle's language in this passage, derived from the
jargon of scholastic logic and philosophy, is designed to confuse Kastril.
Books had been written setting forth for the gallants of the time the
etiquette of quarrelling. 31 **angry** swaggering 44 **myrobolane** sugar
plum 45 **rivo frontis** frontal vein 49 **linea . . . annularis** terms in palmistry

KASTRIL   Hold your peace.
Here comes the tother rare man.—'Save you, Captain.
    FACE   Good master Kastril! Is this your sister?
    KASTRIL   Ay, sir.
Please you to kuss her, and be proud to know her.
    FACE   I shall be proud to know you, lady.
                    [*Kisses her.*]
                                        Brother,
    DAME PLIANT
He calls me lady, too.
    KASTRIL   Ay, peace; I heard it.
                    [*Takes her aside.*]
    FACE   The count is come.
    SUBTLE   Where is he?
    FACE   At the door.
    SUBTLE   Why, you must entertain him.
    FACE   What'll you do   60
With these the while?
    SUBTLE   Why, have 'em up, and show 'em
Some fustian book, or the dark glass.
    FACE   'Fore God,
She is a delicate dabchick! I must have her.   [*Exit.*]
    SUBTLE [*Aside.*]   Must you! Ay, if your fortune will,
        you must.—
Come, sir, the Captain will come to us presently.
I'll ha' you to my chamber of demonstrations,
Where I'll show you both the grammar and logic
And rhetoric of quarreling; my whole method
Drawn out in tables; and my instrument,
That hath the several scale upon't shall make you   70
Able to quarrel at a straw's-breadth by moonlight.
And, lady, I'll have you look in a glass,
Some half an hour, but to clear your eyesight,
Against you see your fortune; which is greater
Than I may judge upon the sudden, trust me.
                                        [*Exeunt.*]

SCENE III

[*Enter* FACE.]

[FACE]   Where are you, Doctor?
    SUBTLE [*Within.*]   I'll come to you presently.
62 **fustian** high-sounding, incomprehensible **dark glass** magic crystal

FACE   I will ha' this same widow, now I ha' seen her,
On any composition.

[*Enter* SUBTLE.]

SUBTLE   What do you say?
FACE   Ha' you dispos'd of them?
SUBTLE   I ha' sent 'em up.
FACE   Subtle, in troth, I needs must have this widow.
SUBTLE   Is that the matter?
FACE   Nay, but hear me.
SUBTLE   Go to.
If you rebel once, Dol shall know it all.
Therefore be quiet, and obey your chance.
10   FACE   Nay, thou art so violent now. Do but conceive,
Thou art old, and canst not serve—
SUBTLE   Who cannot? I?
'Slight, I will serve her with thee, for a—
FACE   Nay,
But understand; I'll gi' you composition.
SUBTLE   I will not treat with thee. What! sell my fortune?
'Tis better than my birthright. Do not murmur.
Win her, and carry her. If you grumble, Dol
Knows it directly.
FACE   Well, sir, I am silent.
Will you go help to fetch in Don in state?   [*Exit.*]
SUBTLE   I follow you, sir. We must keep Face in awe,
20 Or he will overlook us like a tyrant.

[*Re-enter* FACE, *ushering in* SURLY, *who is disguised in the
elaborate costume of a Spanish nobleman.*]

Brain of a tailor! who comes here? Don John!
SURLY   *Señores, beso las manos à vuestras mercedes.*
SUBTLE   Would you had stopp'd a little, and kiss'd our *anos.*
FACE   Peace, Subtle!
SUBTLE   Stab me; I shall never hold, man.
He looks in that deep ruff like a head in a platter,
Serv'd in by a short cloak upon two trestles.
FACE   Or what do you say to a collar of brawn, cut down
Beneath the souse, and wriggled with a knife?
SUBTLE   'Slud, he does look too fat to be a Spaniard.
30   FACE   Perhaps some Fleming or some Hollander got him

4 composition terms   20 overlook dominate   22 Señores . . . mercedes
Gentlemen, I kiss your worships' hands (Spanish).   27 brawn boar's
flesh   28 souse ear

In d'Alva's time; Count Egmont's bastard.

SUBTLE   Don,
Your scurvy, yellow, Madrid face is welcome.

SURLY   *Gratia.*

SUBTLE   He speaks out of a fortification.
Pray God he ha' no squibs in those deeps sets.

SURLY   *Por dios, señores, muy linda casa!*

SUBTLE   What says he?

FACE   Praises the house, I think;
I know no more but's action.

SUBTLE   Yes, the *casa,*
My precious Diego, will prove fair enough
To cozen you in. Do you mark? You shall
Be cozened, Diego.

FACE   Cozened, do you see,   40
My worthy Donzel, cozened.

SURLY   *Entiendo.*

SUBTLE   Do you intend it? So do we, dear Don.
Have you brought pistolets or portagues,
My solemn Don? [*To* FACE.] Dost thou feel any?

                    He feels his pockets.

                                             Full.
FACE
SUBTLE   You shall be emptied, Don, pumped and drawn
Dry, as they say.

FACE   Milked, in troth, sweet Don.

SUBTLE   See all the monsters; the great lion of all, Don.

SURLY   *Con licencia, se puede ver à esta señora?*

SUBTLE   What talks he now?

FACE   O' the señora.

SUBTLE   O, Don,
That is the lioness, which you shall see   50
Also, my Don.

FACE   'Slid, Subtle, how shall we do?

SUBTLE   For what?

FACE   Why, Dol's employ'd, you know.

SUBTLE   That's true.
'Fore heav'n I know not: he must stay, that's all.

FACE   Stay! that he must not by no means.

---

31 d'Alva governor of the Netherlands, 1567-1573 Egmont a Flemish
patriot executed by Alva 33 Gratia thanks 34 sets plaits of his ruff
35 Por . . . casa By God, sirs, a very pretty house. 40 Diego Spaniard
41 Donzel little don Entiendo I understand. 48 Con . . . señora If
you please, may I see the lady?

SUBTLE   No! why?
FACE   Unless you'll mar all. 'Slight, he'll suspect it;
And then he will not pay, not half so well.
This is a travell'd punk-master, and does know
All the delays; a notable hot rascal,
And looks already rampant.
60   SUBTLE   'Sdeath, and Mammon
Must not be troubled.
FACE   Mammon! in no case.
SUBTLE   What shall we do then?
FACE   Think: you must be sudden.
SURLY   *Entiendo que la señora es tan hermosa, que codìcio
tan à verla como la bien aventuránça de mi vida.*
FACE   *Mi vida!* 'Slid, Subtle, he puts me in mind o'
the widow.
What dost thou say to draw her to 't, ha!
And tell her it is her fortune? All our venter
Now lies upon 't. It is but one man more,
70   Which on's chance to have her: and beside,
There is no maidenhead to be fear'd or lost.
What dost thou think on 't, Subtle?
SUBTLE   Who, I? why—
FACE   The credit of our house, too, is engag'd.
SUBTLE   You made me an offer for my share erewhile.
What wilt thou gi' me, i'faith?
FACE   O, by that light,
I'll not buy now. You know your doom to me.
E'en take your lot, obey your chance, sir; win her,
And wear her—out for me.
SUBTLE   'Slight, I'll not work her then.
FACE   It is the common cause; therefore bethink you.
Dol else must know it, as you said.
80   SUBTLE   I care not.
SURLY   *Señores, porque se tarda tanto?*
SUBTLE   Faith, I am not fit, I am old.
FACE   That's now no reason, sir.
SURLY   *Puede ser de hazer burla de mi amor?*
FACE   You hear the Don too? By this air, I call,

63 **Entiendo . . . vida** I understand that the lady is so beautiful that I
am as anxious about seeing her as about the good fortune of my life.
76 **doom** decision   81 **Señores . . . tanto** Sirs, why so much delay?
83 **Puede . . . amor** Can it be to make fun of my love?

And loose the hinges. Dol!

SUBTLE   A plague of hell—

FACE   Will you then do?

SUBTLE   Y'are a terrible rogue!
I'll think of this. Will you, sir, call the widow?

FACE   Yes, and I'll take her, too, with all her faults,
Now I do think on't better.

SUBTLE   With all my heart, sir;
Am I discharg'd o' the lot?

FACE   As you please.

SUBTLE   Hands.   90
                          [*They shake hands.*]

FACE   Remember now, that upon any change
You never claim her.

SUBTLE   Much good joy and health to you, sir.
Marry a whore! Fate, let me wed a witch first.

SURLY   *Por estas honradas barbas—*

SUBTLE   He swears by his beard.
Dispatch, and call the brother, too.   [*Exit* FACE.]

SURLY   *Tengo duda, señores' que no me hágan alguna traycion.*

SUBTLE   How, issue on? Yes, *præsto, señor.* Please you   100
Enthratha the *chambratha,* worthy Don,
Where if you please the fates, in your *bathada,*
You shall be soak'd, and strok'd, and tubb'd, and rubb'd,
And scrubb'd, and fubb'd, dear Don, before you go.
You shall in faith, my scurvy baboon Don,
Be curried, claw'd, and flaw'd, and taw'd, indeed.
I will the heartilier go about it now,
And make the widow a punk so much the sooner,
To be reveng'd on this impetuous Face:
The quickly doing of it is the grace.
                      [*Exeunt* SUBTLE *and* SURLY.]

---

95 Por . . . barbas by this honored beard   97 Tengo . . . traycion I fear,
sirs, you are playing me some foul trick.   103 fubb'd cheated   105 flaw'd
cracked, damaged   taw'd soaked

Scene IV

[Re-enter FACE, *accompanied by Kastril and his sister,*
DAME PLIANT.]

[FACE] Come, lady. [*To Kastril.*] I knew the Doctor would
    not leave
Till he had found the very nick of her fortune.

KASTRIL   To be a countess, say you?

FACE   A Spanish countess, sir.

DAME PLIANT   Why, is that better than an English countess?

FACE   Better! 'Slight, make you that a question, lady?

KASTRIL   Nay, she is a fool, Captain, you must pardon her.

FACE   Ask him from your courtier to your inns-of-court-
man,
To your mere milliner; they will tell you all,
10 Your Spanish jennet is the best horse; your Spanish
Stoop is the best garb; your Spanish beard
Is the best cut; your Spanish ruffs are the best
Wear; your Spanish pavin the best dance;
Your Spanish titillation in a glove
The best perfume; and for your Spanish pike
And Spanish blade, let your poor captain speak.—
Here comes the Doctor.

[Enter SUBTLE *with a paper.]*

SUBTLE   My most honour'd lady,
For so I am now to style you, having found
By this my scheme, you are to undergo
20 An honourable fortune very shortly,
What will you say now, if some—

FACE   I ha' told her all, sir,
And her right worshipful brother here, that she shall be
A countess; do not delay 'em, sir; a Spanish countess.

SUBTLE   Still, my scarce-worshipful captain, you can keep
No secret! Well, since he has told you, madam,
Do you forgive him, and I do.

KASTRIL   She shall do that, sir;
I'll look to't; 'tis my charge.

SUBTLE   Well, then, nought rests
But that she fit her love now to her fortune.

DAME PLIANT   Truly I shall never brook a Spaniard.

11 **garb** bodily carriage 19 **scheme** horoscope

SUBTLE No?

DAME PLIANT Never sin' eighty-eight could I abide 'em,
And that was some three year afore I was born, in truth.

SUBTLE Come, you must love him, or be miserable;
Choose which you will.

FACE By this good rush, persuade her.
She will cry strawberries else within this twelvemonth.

SUBTLE Nay, shads and mackerel, which is worse.

FACE Indeed, sir!

KASTRIL God's lid, you shall love him, or I'll kick you.

DAME PLIANT Why,
I'll do as you will ha' me, brother.

KASTRIL Do, 40
Or by this hand I'll maul you.

FACE Nay, good sir,
Be not so fierce.

SUBTLE No, my enraged child;
She will be rul'd. What, when she comes to taste
The pleasures of a countess! to be courted—

FACE And kiss'd and ruffled!

SUBTLE Ay, behind the hangings.

FACE And then come forth in pomp!

SUBTLE And know her state!

FACE Of keeping all th' idolators o' the chamber
Barer to her, than at their prayers!

SUBTLE Is serv'd
Upon the knee!

FACE And has her pages, ushers,
Footmen, and coaches—

SUBTLE Her six mares—

FACE Nay, eight! 50

SUBTLE To hurry her through London, to th' Exchange,
Bet'lem, the China-houses—

FACE Yes, and have
The citizens gape at her, and praise her tires,
And my lord's goose-turd bands, that rides with her!

KASTRIL Most brave! By this hand, you are not my suster
If you refuse.

---

31 **eighty-eight** 1588, the year of the defeat of the Spanish Armada
34 **rush** the floor of the stage was covered with rushes 35 **cry hawk** on
the street 51 **Exchange** a shopping center 52 **Bet'lem** Bethlehem Hospital for the insane, which was visited for amusement **China-houses**
shops for the sale of Oriental goods 54 **goose-turd** greenish-yellow

DAME PLIANT I will not refuse, brother.

[Enter SURLY.*]*

SURLY *Que es esto, señores, que non se venga?*
Esta tardanza me mata!

FACE It is the count come!
60 The Doctor knew he would be here, by his art.

SUBTLE *En gallanta madama, Don! gallantissima!*

SURLY *Por todos los dioses, la mas acabada*
Hermosura, que he visto en mi vida!

FACE Is't not a gallant language that they speak?

KASTRIL An admirable language! Is't not French?

FACE No, Spanish, sir.

KASTRIL It goes like law French,
And that, they say, is the courtliest language.

FACE List, sir.

SURLY *El sol ha perdido su lumbre, con el*
Resplandor que tràe esta dama! Valga me dios!

FACE H'admires your sister.

70 KASTRIL Must not she make curt'sy?

SUBTLE 'Ods will, she must go to him, man, and kiss him!
It is the Spanish fashion, for the women
To make first court.

FACE 'Tis true he tells you, sir;
His art knows all.

SURLY *Porque no se acùde?*

KASTRIL He speaks to her, I think.

FACE That he does, sir.

SURLY *Por el amor de dios, que es esto que se tàrda?*

KASTRIL Nay, see: she will not understand him! **Gull,**
noddy!

DAME PLIANT What say you, brother?

KASTRIL Ass, my suster,
80 Go kuss him, as the cunning man would ha' you;
I'll thrust a pin i' your buttocks else.

FACE O no, sir.

---

58 **Que . . . mata** Why does she not come, sirs? This delay is killing
me. 62 **Por . . . vida** By all the gods, the most perfect beauty that I
have seen in my life! 66 **law French** the official court language for
centuries 68 **El . . . dios** The sun has lost his light with the splendor
this lady brings, so help me God. 74 **Porque . . . acude** Why do you not
draw near? 76 **Por . . . tarda** For the love of God, why this delay?

SURLY *Señora mia, mi persona muy indigna està*
Allegar à tanta hermosura.

FACE Does he not use her bravely?

KASTRIL Bravely, i' faith!

FACE Nay, he will use her better.

KASTRIL Do you think so?

SURLY *Señora, si sera servida, entremos.*

[*Exit with* DAME PLIANT.]

KASTRIL Where does he carry her?

FACE Into the garden, sir;
Take you no thought. I must interpret for her.

SUBTLE [*Aside to* FACE.] Give Dol the word.

[*Exit* FACE.]
—Come, my fierce child, advance,
We'll to our quarrelling lesson again.

KASTRIL Agreed. 90
I love a Spanish boy with all my heart.

SUBTLE Nay, and by this means, sir, you shall be brother
To a great count.

KASTRIL Ay, I knew that at first.
This match will advance the house of the Kastrils.

SUBTLE 'Pray God your sister prove but pliant!

KASTRIL Why,
Her name is so, by her other husband.

SUBTLE How!

KASTRIL The Widow Pliant. Knew you not that?

SUBTLE No, faith, sir;
Yet, by the erection of her figure, I guess'd it.
Come, let's go practise.

KASTRIL Yes, but do you think, Doctor,
I e'er shall quarrel well?

SUBTLE I warrant you. [*Exeunt.*] 100

82 Señora . . . hermosura My lady, my person is most unworthy to
approach such beauty. 86 Señora . . . entremos Madam, if you please,
let us go in. 98 figure horoscope (with an obvious pun)

Scene V

[Enter DOL, *in her fit of violent talking, followed
by* MAMMON.]

[DOL COMMON]   For, after Alexander's death—
MAMMON   Good lady—
DOL COMMON   That Perdiccas and Antigonus were slain,
The two that stood, Seleuc' and Ptolemy—
MAMMON   Madam—
DOL COMMON   Made up the two legs, and the fourth beast,
That was Gog-north and Egypt-south: which after
Was call'd Gog-iron-leg and South-iron-leg—
MAMMON   Lady—
DOL COMMON   And then Gog-horned. So was Egypt, too:
Then Egypt-clay-leg, and Gog-clay-leg—
MAMMON   Sweet madam—
DOL COMMON   And last Gog-dust, and Egypt-dust, which
10 fall
In the last link of the fourth chain. And these
Be stars in story, which none see, or look at—
MAMMON   What shall I do?
DOL COMMON   For, as he says, except
We call the rabbins, and the heathen Greeks—
MAMMON   Dear lady—
DOL COMMON   To come from Salem, and from Athens,
And teach the people of Great Britain—

[Enter FACE *hastily, in his laboratory assistant's dress.]*

FACE   What's the matter, sir?
DOL COMMON   To speak the tongue of Eber and Javan—
MAMMON   O,
She's in her fit.
DOL COMMON   We shall know nothing—
20   FACE   Death, sir,
We are undone!
DOL COMMON   Where then a learned linguist
Shall see the ancient us'd communion

---

1 s.d. fit of talking Face had told Mammon (II, 3, 251-56) that Dol
was being treated for madness. She raves whenever anything touching
the Hebrew scriptures is mentioned. Jonson has composed Dol's ravings
in the following passage from Hugh Broughton's *Concent of Scripture*,
somewhat garbled for comic effect. The empire of Alexander played an
important part in Broughton's interpretation of the Bible.

Of vowels and consonants—

FACE My master will hear!

DOL COMMON A wisdom, which Pythagoras held most high—

MAMMON Sweet honourable lady!

DOL COMMON To comprise
All sounds of voices, in few marks of letters.

FACE Nay, you must never hope to lay her now.

They speak together.

DOL COMMON And so we may arrive by Talmud skill, 30
And profane Greek, to raise the building up
Of Helen's house against the Ismaelite,
King of Thogarma, and his habergions
Brimstony, blue, and fiery; and the force
Of king Abaddon, and the beast of Cittim:
Which rabbi David Kimchi, Onkelos,
And Aben Ezra do interpret Rome.

FACE How did you put her into't?

MAMMON Alas, I talk'd
Of a fift monarchy I would erect
With the philosopher's stone, by chance, and she 40
Falls on the other four straight.

FACE Out of Broughton!
I told you so. 'Slid, stop her mouth.

MAMMON Is't best?

FACE She'll never leave else. If the old man hear her,
We are but *fæces,* ashes.

SUBTLE [*Within.*] What's to do there?

FACE O, we are lost! Now she hears him, she is quiet.

[*Enter* SUBTLE. MAMMON *stands aghast. Exeunt*
FACE *and* DOLL.]

MAMMON Where shall I hide me!

SUBTLE How! What sight is here?
Close deeds of darkness, and that shun the light!
Bring him again. Who is he? What, my son!
O, I have liv'd too long.

MAMMON Nay, good, dear father, 50
There was no unchaste purpose.

SUBTLE Not? and flee me
When I come in?

29 *i.e.,* Dol continues to rave while Mammon and Face speak. 48 Close
secret

MAMMON   That was my error.

SUBTLE   Error?
Guilt, guilt, my son; give it the right name. No marvel
If I found check in our great work within,
When such affairs as these were managing!

MAMMON   Why, have you so?

SUBTLE   It has stood still this half hour,
And all the rest of our less works gone back.
Where is the instrument of wickedness,
My lewd false drudge?

MAMMON   Nay, good sir, blame not him;
60 Believe me, 'twas against his will or knowledge.
I saw her by chance.

SUBTLE   Will you commit more sin,
T'excuse a varlet?

MAMMON   By my hope, 'tis true, sir.

SUBTLE   Nay, then I wonder less, if you, for whom
The blessing was prepar'd, would so tempt heaven,
And lose your fortunes.

MAMMON   Why, sir?

SUBTLE   This'll retard
The work a month at least.

MAMMON   Why, if it do,
What remedy? But think it not, good father;
Our purposes were honest.

SUBTLE   As they were,
So the reward will prove.   *A great crack and*
70   How now! ay me!   *noise within.*
God and all saints be good to us.—

[*Re-enter* FACE.]

What's that?
FACE   O, sir, we are defeated! All the works
Are flown *in fumo,* every glass is burst!
Furnace and all rent down, as if a bolt
Of thunder had been driven through the house.
Retorts, receivers, pelicans, bolt-heads,
All struck in shivers!   SUBTLE *falls down,*
Help, good sir! alas,   *as in a swoon.*
Coldness and death invades him. Nay, Sir Mammon,
80 Do the fair offices of a man! You stand,
As you were readier to depart than he.

68 honest chaste   73 in fumo in smoke   77 shivers splinters

One knocks.

Who's there? My lord her brother is come.

MAMMON   Ha, Lungs!

FACE   His coach is at the door. Avoid his sight,
For he's as furious as his sister is mad.

MAMMON   Alas!

FACE   My brain is quite undone with the fume, sir,
I ne'er must hope to be mine own man again.

MAMMON   Is all lost, Lungs? Will nothing be preserv'd
Of all our cost?

FACE   Faith, very little, sir;
A peck of coals or so, which is cold comfort, sir.

MAMMON   O, my voluptuous mind! I am justly punish'd.   90

FACE   And so am I, sir.

MAMMON   Cast from all my hopes—

FACE   Nay, certainties, sir.

MAMMON   By mine own base affections.

                              SUBTLE *seems come to himself.*

SUBTLE   O, the curst fruits of vice and lust!

MAMMON   Good father,
It was my sin. Forgive it.

SUBTLE   Hangs my roof
Over us still, and will not fall, O Justice,
Upon us, for this wicked man!

FACE   Nay, look, sir,
You grieve him now with staying in his sight.
Good sir, the nobleman will come too, and take you,
And that may breed a tragedy.

MAMMON   I'll go.

FACE   Ay, and repent at home, sir. It may be,   100
For some good penance you may ha' it yet;
A hundred pound to the box at Bet'lem—

MAMMON   Yes.

FACE   For the restoring such as ha' their wits.

MAMMON   I'll do't.

FACE   I'll send one to you to receive it.

MAMMON   Do.
Is no projection left?

FACE   All flown, or stinks, sir.

MAMMON   Will nought be sav'd that's good for med'cine,
   think'st thou?

FACE   I cannot tell, sir. There will be perhaps
Something about the scraping of the shards,

110 Will cure the itch,—though not your itch of mind, sir.
It shall be sav'd for you, and sent home. Good sir,
This way, for fear the lord should meet you.

                                                             [Exit MAMMON.]

SUBTLE [*Raising his head.*]   Face!

FACE   Ay.

SUBTLE   Is he gone?

FACE   Yes, and as heavily
As all the gold he hop'd for were in his blood.
Let us be light though.

SUBTLE [*Leaping up.*]   Ay, as balls, and bound
And hit our heads against the roof for joy:
There's so much of our care now cast away.

FACE   Now to our Don.

120   SUBTLE   Yes, your young widow by this time
Is made a countess, Face; she's been in travail
Of a young heir for you.

FACE   Good, sir.

SUBTLE   Off with your case,
And greet her kindly, as a bridegroom should,
After these common hazards.

FACE   Very well, sir.
Will you go fetch Don Diego off the while?

SUBTLE   And fetch him over too, if you'll be pleas'd, sir.
Would Dol were in her place, to pick his pockets now!

FACE   Why, you can do it as well, if you would set to't.
I pray you prove your virtue.

SUBTLE   For your sake, sir.   *[Exeunt.]*

SCENE VI

[*Enter* SURLY, *still in his Spanish nobleman's costume,
and* DAME PLIANT.]

[SURLY]   Lady, you see into what hands you are fall'n;
'Mongst what a nest of villains! and how near
Your honour was t'have catch'd a certain clap,
Through your credulity, had I but been
So punctually forward, as place, time,
And other circumstance would ha' made a man;
For y'are a handsome woman: would you were wise too!

122 case his laboratory assistant's costume 129 virtue power, ability

I am a gentleman come here disguis'd,
Only to find the knaveries of this citadel;
And where I might have wrong'd your honour, and have not, 10
I claim some interest in your love. You are,
They say, a widow, rich; and I'm a bachelor,
Worth nought. Your fortunes may make me a man,
As mine ha' preserv'd you a woman. Think upon it,
And whether I have deserv'd you or no.

DAME PLIANT   I will, sir.
SURLY   And for these household-rogues, let me alone
To treat with them.

                    [*Enter* SUBTLE.]

SUBTLE   How doth my noble Diego,
And my dear madam Countess? Hath the Count
Been courteous, lady? liberal and open?
Donzel, methinks you look melancholic,   20
After your *coitum,* and scurvy! Truly,
I do not like the dulness of your eye;
It hath a heavy cast, 'tis upsee Dutch,
And says you are a lumpish whore-master.
Be lighter, I will make your pockets so.
                He falls to picking of them.
SURLY   Will you, Don Bawd and Pick-purse?
            [*Knocks him down.*]   How now! Reel you?
Stand up, sir, you shall find, since I am so heavy,
I'll gi' you equal weight.
SUBTLE   Help! murder!
SURLY   No, sir,
There's no such thing intended. A good cart
And a clean whip shall ease you of that fear.   30
I am the Spanish Don that should be cozened,
Do you see? Cozened? Where's your Captain Face,
That parcel-broker, and whole-bawd, all rascal?

            [*Enter* FACE *in his uniform.*]

FACE   How, Surly!
SURLY   O, make your approach, good Captain.
I've found from whence your copper rings and spoons
Come now, wherewith you cheat abroad in taverns.
'Twas here you learn'd t'anoint your boot with brimstone,

23 upsee Dutch thoroughly Dutch(?)   30 whip bawds were whipped
through town at the tail of a cart.   33 parcel part

Then rub men's gold on't for a kind of touch,
40 And say 'twas naught, when you had chang'd the colour,
That you might ha't for nothing. And this Doctor,
Your sooty, smoky-bearded compeer, he
Will close you so much gold, in a bolt's-head,
And, on a turn, convey i' the stead another
With sublim'd mercury, that shall burst i' the heat,
And fly out all *in fumo!* Then weeps Mammon;
Then swoons his worship. Or,   [FACE *slips out.*]
        he is the Faustus,
That casteth figures and can conjure, cures
Plagues, piles, and pox, by the ephemerides,
5 And holds intelligence with all the bawds
And midwives of three shires; while you send in—
Captain!—What! is he gone?—damsels with child,
Wives that are barren, or the waiting-maid
With the green sickness.   [*Seizes* SUBTLE *as he is retiring.*]
                —Nay, sir, you must tarry,
Though he be scap'd; and answer by the ears, sir.

SCENE VII

[*Re-enter* FACE *with* KASTRIL.]

[FACE] Why, now's the time, if ever you will quarrel
Well, as they say, and be a true-born child.
The Doctor and your sister both are abus'd.
    KASTRIL Where is he? Which is he? He is a slave,
Whate'er he is, and the son of a whore.—Are you
The man, sir, I would know?
    SURLY   I should be loath, sir,
To confess so much.
    KASTRIL   Then you lie i' your throat.
    SURLY   How!
    FACE [*To* KASTRIL.]   A very arrant rogue, sir,
    and a cheater,
Employ'd here by another conjurer
10 That does not love the Doctor, and would cross him,
If he knew how.
    SURLY   Sir, you are abus'd.
    KASTRIL   You lie:

49 ephemerides astrological almanacs

And 'tis no matter.

    FACE   Well said, sir! He is

The impudent'st rascal—

    SURLY   You are indeed. Will you hear me, sir?

    FACE   By no means. Bid him be gone.

    KASTRIL   Begone, sir, quickly.

    SURLY   This's strange! Lady, do you inform your brother.

    FACE   There is not such a foist in all the town.

The Doctor had him presently; and finds yet

The Spanish Count will come here.—[*Aside.*] Bear up,
    Subtle.

    SUBTLE   Yes, sir, he must appear within this hour.   **20**

    FACE   And yet this rogue would come in a disguise,

By the temptation of another spirit,

To trouble our art, though he could not hurt it.

    KASTRIL   Ay,

I know—[*to his sister.*] Away, you talk like a foolish
    mauther.

    SURLY   Sir, all is truth she says.

    FACE   Do not believe him, sir.

He is the lying'st swabber! Come your ways, sir.

    SURLY   You are valiant out of company!

    KASTRIL   Yes, how then, sir?

    [*Enter* DRUGGER *with a piece of damask.*]

    FACE   Nay, here's an honest fellow too that knows him,

And all his tricks.—[*Aside to* DRUGGER.] Make good what I
    say, Abel;

This cheater would ha' cozen'd thee o' the widow.—   **30**

He owes this honest Drugger here seven pound,

He has had on him in twopenny'orths of tobacco.

    DRUGGER   Yes, sir. And's damn'd himself three terms
    to pay me.

    FACE   And what does he owe for lotium?

    DRUGGER   Thirty shillings, sir;

And for six syringes.

    SURLY   Hydra of villainy!

    FACE   Nay, sir, you must quarrel him out o' the house.

    KASTRIL   I will.

—Sir, if you get not out o' doors, you lie;

And you are a pimp.

17 **foist** crook 24 **mauther** wench 27 **out of company when you are**
alone

SURLY   Why, this is madness, sir,
40 Not valour in you. I must laugh at this.
    KASTRIL   It is my humour; you are a pimp and a trig,
And an Amadis de Gaul, or a Don Quixote.
    DRUGGER   Or a knight o' the curious coxcomb, do you see?

[*Enter* ANANIAS.]

    ANANIAS   Peace to the household!
    KASTRIL   I'll keep peace for no man.
    ANANIAS   Casting of dollars is concluded lawful.
    KASTRIL   Is he the constable?
    SUBTLE   Peace, Ananias.
    FACE   No, sir.
    KASTRIL   Then you are an otter, and a shad, a whit,
A very tim.
    SURLY   You'll hear me, sir?
    KASTRIL   I will not.
    ANANIAS   What is the motive?
    SUBTLE   Zeal in the young gentleman,
Against his Spanish slops.
50 ANANIAS   They are profane,
Lewd, superstitious, and idolatrous breeches.
    SURLY   New rascals!
    KASTRIL   Will you be gone, sir?
    ANANIAS   Avoid, Sathan!
Thou art not of the light! That ruff of pride
About thy neck betrays thee, and is the same
With that which the unclean birds, in seventy-seven,
Were seen to prank it with on divers coasts:
Thou look'st like Antichrist, in that lewd hat.
    SURLY   I must give way.
    KASTRIL   Be gone, sir.
    SURLY   But I'll take
A course with you—
    ANANIAS   Depart, proud Spanish fiend!
    SURLY   Captain and Doctor—
    ANANIAS   Child of perdition!
60 KASTRIL   Hence, sir!—[*Exit* SURLY.]
Did I not quarrel bravely?
    FACE   Yes, indeed, sir.

41 **trig** coxcomb 42 **Amadis de Gaul** the hero of an old romance of
chivalry 47 **whit, tim** of uncertain meaning 55 **unclean ... seven** unex-
plained allusion

KASTRIL   Nay, an I give my mind to't, I shall do't.

FACE   O, you must follow, sir, and threaten him tame.
He'll turn again else.

KASTRIL   I'll re-turn him then.   [*Exit.*]

FACE   Drugger, this rogue prevented us, for thee.
We had determin'd that thou should'st ha' come
In a Spanish suit, and ha' carried her so; and he,
A brokerly slave, goes, puts it on himself.
Hast brought the damask?

DRUGGER   Yes, sir.

FACE   Thou must borrow
A Spanish suit. Hast thou no credit with the players?   70

DRUGGER   Yes, sir; did you never see me play the Fool?

FACE   I know not, Nab.—[*Aside.*] Thou shalt, if I
can help it.—
Hieronimo's old cloak, ruff, and hat will serve;
I'll tell thee more when thou bring'st 'em.

                                    [*Exit* DRUGGER.]

ANANIAS   *Subtle hath whisper'd with him this while.*
                                Sir, I know
The Spaniard hates the Brethren, and hath spies
Upon their actions; and that this was one
I make no scruple.—But the Holy Synod
Have been in prayer and meditation for it;
And 'tis reveal'd no less to them than me,   80
That casting of money is most lawful.

SUBTLE   True.
But here I cannot do it; if the house
Should chance to be suspected, all would out,
And we be lock'd up in the Tower for ever,
To make gold there for th' state, never come out.
And then are you defeated.

ANANIAS   I will tell
This to the elders and the weaker Brethren,
That the whole company of the Separation
May join in humble prayer again.

SUBTLE   And fasting.

ANANIAS   Yea, for some fitter place. The peace of mind   90
Rest with these walls!

SUBTLE   Thanks, courteous Ananias.

                                [*Exit* ANANIAS.]

FACE   What did he come for?

74 **Hieronimo** character in Kyd's *Spanish Tragedy*

SUBTLE   About casting dollars,
Presently, out of hand. And so I told him,
A Spanish minister came here to spy
Against the faithful—

FACE   I conceive. Come, Subtle,
Thou art so down upon the least disaster!
How wouldst thou ha' done, if I had not help'd thee out?

SUBTLE   I thank thee, Face, for the angry boy, i' faith.

FACE   Who would ha' look'd it should ha' been that rascal
100 Surly? He had dy'd his beard and all. Well, sir,
Heres damask come to make you a suit.

SUBTLE   Where's Drugger?

FACE   He is gone to borrow me a Spanish habit;
I'll be the count now.

SUBTLE   But where's the widow?

FACE   Within, with my lord's sister; Madam Dol
Is entertaining her.

SUBTLE   By your favour, Face,
Now she is honest, I will stand again.

FACE   You will not offer it!

SUBTLE   Why?

FACE   Stand to your word,
Or—here comes Dol!—she knows—

SUBTLE   Y'are tyrannous still.

[*Enter* DOL *hastily.*]

FACE   —Strict for my right.—How now, Dol! Hast
      told her
The Spanish Count will come?

110 DOL COMMON   Yes, but another is come,
You little look'd for!

FACE   Who's that?

DOL COMMON   Your master—
The master of the house.

SUBTLE   How, Dol!

FACE   She lies,
This is some trick. Come, leave your quiblins, Dorothy.

DOL COMMON   Look out and see.

                            [FACE *goes to the window.*]

SUBTLE   Art thou in earnest?

DOL COMMON   'Slight,
Forty o' the neighbours are about him, talking.

99 **look'd** expected   113 **quiblins** quibbles

FACE 'Tis he, by this good day.

DOL COMMON 'Twill prove ill day
For some on us.

FACE We are undone, and taken.

DOL COMMON Lost, I'm afraid.

SUBTLE You said he would not come,
While there died one a week within the liberties.

FACE No: 'twas within the walls.

SUBTLE Was't so? Cry you mercy. 120
I thought the liberties. What shall we do now, Face?

FACE Be silent: not a word, if he call or knock.
I'll into mine old shape again and meet him,
Of Jeremy, the butler. I' the meantime,
Do you two pack up all the goods and purchase
That we can carry i' the two trunks. I'll keep him
Off for to-day, if I cannot longer, and then
At night, I'll ship you both away to Ratcliff,
Where we will meet to-morrow, and there we'll share.
Let Mammon's brass and pewter keep the cellar; 130
We'll have another time for that. But, Dol,
'Pray thee go heat a little water quickly;
Subtle must shave me. All my captain's beard
Must off, to make me appear smooth Jeremy.
You'll do't?

SUBTLE Yes, I'll shave you as well as I can.

FACE And not cut my throat, but trim me?

SUBTLE You shall see, sir. [*Exeunt.*]

119 liberties suburban slum districts of London 125 purchase loot

Act V

[Enter LOVEWIT *with a Crowd of* NEIGHBORS.]

[LOVEWIT]   Has there been such resort, say you?
1 NEIGHBOR   Daily, sir.
2 NEIGHBOR   And nightly, too.
3 NEIGHBOR   Ay, some as brave as lords.
4 NEIGHBOR   Ladies and gentlewomen.
5 NEIGHBOR   Citizens' wives.
1 NEIGHBOR   And knights.
6 NEIGHBOR   In coaches.
2 NEIGHBOR   Yes, and oyster-women.
1 NEIGHBOR   Beside other gallants.
3 NEIGHBOR   Sailors' wives.
4 NEIGHBOR   Tobacco men.
5 NEIGHBOR   Another Pimlico.
LOVEWIT   What should my knave advance,
To draw this company? He hung out no banners
Of a strange calf with five legs to be seen,
Or a huge lobster with six claws?
6 NEIGHBOR   No, sir.
3 NEIGHBOR   We had gone in then, sir.
10 LOVEWIT   He has no gift
Of teaching i' the nose that e'er I knew of.
You saw no bills set up that promis'd cure
Of agues or the tooth-ache?
2 NEIGHBOR   No such thing, sir!
LOVEWIT   Nor heard a drum struck for baboons or puppets?
5 NEIGHBOR   Neither, sir.
LOVEWIT   What device should he bring forth now?
I love a teeming wit as I love my nourishment.
'Pray God he ha' not kept such open house,
That he hath sold my hangings, and my bedding!
I left him nothing else. If he have eat 'em,
20 A plague o' the moth, say I! Sure he has got
Some bawdy pictures to call all this ging:

6 **Pimlico** a popular summer resort, near Hogsden   11 **teaching . . . nose**
i.e., preaching with a nasal whine like a Puritan   12 **bills** posters
21 **ging** gang

The Friar and the Nun; or the new motion
Of the knight's courser covering the parson's mare;
The boy of six year old, with the great thing;
Or 't may be, he has the fleas that run at tilt
Upon a table, or some dog to dance.
When saw you him?

  1 NEIGHBOR   Who, sir, Jeremy?

  2 NEIGHBOR   Jeremy butler?
We saw him not this month.

  LOVEWIT   How!

  4 NEIGHBOR   Not these five weeks, sir.

  [6] NEIGHBOR These six weeks, at the least.

  LOVEWIT   You amaze me, neighbors!

  5 NEIGHBOR Sure, if your worship know not where he is,   30
He's slipp'd away.

  6 NEIGHBOR Pray God he be not made away.

  LOVEWIT Ha! It's no time to question, then.

                              He knocks.

  6 NEIGHBOR   About
Some three weeks since I heard a doleful cry,
As I sat up a-mending my wife's stockings.

  LOVEWIT This's strange that none will answer! Did'st thou
    hear
A cry, sayst thou?

  6 NEIGHBOR   Yes, sir, like unto a man
That had been strangled an hour, and could not speak.

  2 NEIGHBOR I heard it, too, just this day three weeks, at two
o'clock   40
Next morning.

  LOVEWIT These be miracles, or you make 'em so!
A man an hour strangled, and could not speak,
And both you heard him cry?

  3 NEIGHBOR   Yes, downward, sir.

  LOVEWIT Thou art a wise fellow. Give me thy hand, I pray
thee.
What trade art thou on?

  3 NEIGHBOR A smith, an't please your worship.

  LOVEWIT A smith! Then lend me thy help to get this door
open.   50

  3 NEIGHBOR That I will presently, sir, but fetch my tools—

                                          [Exit.]

  1 NEIGHBOR Sir, best to knock again afore you break it.

22 **motion** puppet show

SCENE II

[LOVEWIT *knocks again.*]   I will.

[*Enter* FACE *in his butler's livery.*]

FACE   What mean you, sir?
1, 2, 4 NEIGHBOR   O, here's Jeremy!
FACE   Good sir, come from the door.
LOVEWIT   Why, what's the matter?
FACE   Yet farder, you are too near yet.
LOVEWIT   I' the name of wonder,
What means the fellow!
FACE   The house, sir, has been visited.
LOVEWIT   What, with the plague? Stand thou then farder.
FACE   No, sir,
I had it not.
LOVEWIT   Who had it then? I left
None else but thee i' the house.
FACE   Yes, sir, my fellow,
The cat that kept the buttery, had it on her
10 A week before I spied it; but I got her
Convey'd away i' the night; and so I shut
The house up for a month—
LOVEWIT   How!
FACE   Purposing then, sir,
T'have burnt rose-vinegar, treacle, and tar,
And ha' made it sweet, that you should ne'er ha' known it;
Because I knew the news would but afflict you, sir.
LOVEWIT   Breathe less, and farder off! Why this is stranger:
The neighbours tell me all here that the doors
Have still been open—
FACE   How, sir!
LOVEWIT   Gallants, men and women,
And of all sorts, tag-rag, been seen to flock here
20 In threaves, these ten weeks, as to a second Hogsden,
In days of Pimlico and Eye-bright.
FACE   Sir,
Their wisdoms will not say so.
LOVEWIT   To-day they speak
Of coaches and gallants; one in a French hood
Went in, they tell me; and another was seen

20 **threaves** droves 21 **Eye-bright** a suburban tavern(?)

In a velvet gown at the windore; divers more
Pass in and out.

FACE   They did pass through the doors then,
Or walls, I assure their eye-sights, and their spectacles;
For here, sir, are the keys, and here have been,
In this my pocket, now above twenty days!
And for before, I kept the fort alone there.   30
But that 'tis yet not deep i' the afternoon,
I should believe my neighbours had seen double
Through the black pot, and made these apparitions!
For, on my faith to your worship, for these three weeks
And upwards, the door has not been open'd.

LOVEWIT   Strange!

1 NEIGHBOR   Good faith, I think I saw a coach.

2 NEIGHBOR   And I too,
I'd ha' been sworn.

LOVEWIT   Do you but think it now?
And but one coach?

4 NEIGHBOR   We cannot tell, sir; Jeremy
Is a very honest fellow.

FACE   Did you see me at all?

1 NEIGHBOR   No; that we are sure on.

2 NEIGHBOR   I'll be sworn o' that.   40

LOVEWIT   Fine rogues to have your testimonies built on!

[*Re-enter Third* NEIGHBOR, *with his tools.*]

3 NEIGHBOR   Is Jeremy come!

1 NEIGHBOR   O yes; you may leave your tools;
We were deceiv'd, he says.

2 NEIGHBOR   He's had the keys,
And the door has been shut these three weeks.

3 NEIGHBOR   Like enough.

LOVEWIT   Peace, and get hence, you changelings.

[*Enter* SURLY *and* MAMMON.]

FACE [*Aside.*]   Surly come!
And Mammon made acquainted! They'll tell all.
How shall I beat them off? What shall I do?
Nothing's more wretched than a guilty conscience.

33 **Through** . . . **pot** from drinking too much

SCENE III

[SURLY]   No, sir, he was a great physician. This,
It was no bawdy-house, but a mere chancel!
You knew the lord and his sister.
 MAMMON   Nay, good Surly.
 SURLY The happy word, *be rich*—
 MAMMON   Play not the tyrant.
 SURLY Should be to-day pronounc'd to all your friends.
And where be your andirons now? And your brass pots,
That should ha' been golden flagons, and great wedges?
 MAMMON Let me but breathe. What, they ha' shut their
doors,
10 Methinks!   MAMMON *and* SURLY *knock*.
 SURLY Ay, now 'tis holiday with them.
 MAMMON   Rogues,
Cozeners, impostors, bawds!
 FACE   What mean you, sir?
 MAMMON To enter if we can.
 FACE   Another man's house!
Here is the owner, sir; turn you to him,
And speak your business.
 MAMMON   Are you, sir, the owner?
 LOVEWIT Yes, sir.
 MAMMON And are those knaves, within, your cheaters?
 LOVE What knaves, what cheaters?
 MAMMON   Subtle and his Lungs.
 FACE The gentleman is distracted, sir! No lungs
20 Nor lights ha' been seen here these three weeks, sir,
Within these doors, upon my word.
 SURLY   Your word,
Groom arrogant!
 FACE   Yes, sir. I am the housekeeper,
And know the keys ha' not been out o' my hands.
 SURLY This's a new Face.
 FACE   You do mistake the house, sir.
What sign was't at?
 SURLY   You rascal! This is one
O' the confederacy. Come, let's get officers,
And force the door.
 LOVEWIT Pray you stay, gentlemen.
 SURLY No, sir, we'll come with warrant.
 MAMMON   Ay, and then

We shall ha' your doors open.

                          [Exeunt MAMMON *and* SURLY.]

LOVEWIT   What means this?

FACE   I cannot tell, sir.

1 NEIGHBOR   These are two o' the gallants   30

That we do think we saw.

FACE   Two o' the fools!

You talk as idly as they. Good faith, sir,

I think the moon has craz'd 'em all.   *[Enter* KASTRIL.]

     [Aside.] O me,

The angry boy come too! He'll make a noise,

And ne'er away till he have betray'd us all.

                                 KASTRIL *knocks.*

KASTRIL   What, rogues, bawds, slaves, you'll open the door

anon!

Punk, cockatrice, my suster! By this light,

I'll fetch the marshal to you. You are a whore

To keep your castle—

FACE   Who would you speak with, sir?   40

KASTRIL   The bawdy Doctor, and the cozening Captain,

And puss my suster.

LOVEWIT   This is something, sure.

FACE   Upon my trust, the doors were never open, sir.

KASTRIL   I have heard all their tricks told me twice over,

By the fat knight and the lean gentleman.

LOVEWIT   Here comes another.

          [Enter ANANIAS *and* TRIBULATION.]

FACE   Ananias too!

And his pastor!

TRIBULATION   The doors are shut against us.

          They beat, too, at the door.

ANANIAS   Come forth, you seed of sulphur, sons of fire!

Your stench it is broke forth; abomination   50

Is in the house.

KASTRIL   Ay, my suster's there.

ANANIAS   The place,

It is become a cage of unclean birds.

KASTRIL   Yes, I will fetch the scavenger, and the constable.

TRIBULATION   You shall do well.

ANANIAS   We'll join to weed them out.

KASTRIL   You will not come then, punk devise, my suster!

38 **cockatrice** prostitute 55 **punk devise** perfect harlot

ANANIAS Call her not sister; she is a harlot verily.

KASTRIL I'll raise the street.

LOVEWIT   Good gentlemen, a word.

ANANIAS Sathan, avoid, and hinder not our zeal!

[*Exeunt* ANANIAS, TRIBULATION, *and* KASTRIL.]

LOVEWIT The world's turn'd Bet'lem.

FACE   These are all broke loose,

60 Out of St. Katherine's, where they use to keep
The better sort of mad-folks.

1 NEIGHBOR   All these persons
We saw go in and out here.

2 NEIGHBOR   Yes, indeed, sir.

3 NEIGHBOR These were the parties.

FACE   Peace, you drunkards! Sir,
I wonder at it. Please you to give me leave
To touch the door; I'll try an the lock be chang'd.

LOVEWIT It mazes me!

FACE [*Goes to the door.*] Good faith, sir, I believe
There's no such thing; 'tis all *deceptio visus*—
[*Aside.*] Would I could get him away.

[DAPPER *cries out within.*]

70   DAPPER Master Captain! Master Doctor!

LOVEWIT Who's that?

FACE [*Aside.*] Our clerk within, that I forgot!—
I know not, sir.

DAPPER [*Within.*] For God's sake, when will her Grace be
at leisure?

FACE   Ha!
Illusions, some spirit o' the air!—[*Aside.*] His gag is melted,
And now he sets out the throat.

DAPPER [*Within.*]   I am almost stifled—

FACE [*Aside.*] Would you were altogether.

LOVE   'Tis i' the house.
Ha! list.

FACE Believe it, sir, i' the air.

LOVEWIT   Peace, you.

DAPPER [*Within.*] Mine aunt's grace does not use me well.

SUBTLE [*Within.*]   You fool,
80 Peace, you'll mar all.

FACE [*Speaks through the keyhole, unaware that* LOVEWIT
has tiptoed up behind him and overhears.] Or you will else,
you rogue.

68 deceptio visus optical illusion

LOVEWIT   O, is it so? Then you converse with spirits!—
Come, sir. No more o' your tricks, good Jeremy.
The truth, the shortest way.

FACE   Dismiss this rabble, sir.—
[*Aside*.]   What shall I do? I am catch'd.

LOVEWIT   Good neighbours,
I thank you all. You may depart. [*Exeunt* NEIGHBORS.]—
Come, sir,
You know that I am an indulgent master;
And therefore conceal nothing. What's your med'cine,   90
To draw so many several sorts of wild fowl?

FACE   Sir, you were wont to affect mirth and wit—
But here's no place to talk on't i' the street.
Give me but leave to make the best of my fortune,
And only pardon me th' abuse of your house:
It's all I beg. I'll help you to a widow,
In recompense, that you shall gi' me thanks for,
Will make you seven years younger, and a rich one.
'Tis but your putting on a Spanish cloak;
I have her within. You need not fear the house;   100
It was not visited.

LOVEWIT   But by me, who came
Sooner than you expected.

FACE   It is true, sir.
'Pray you forgive me.

LOVEWIT   Well, let's see your widow.   [*Exeunt.*]

Scene IV

[*Enter* SUBTLE, *leading in* DAPPER, *with his eyes bound
as before.*]

[SUBTLE]   How! ha' you eaten your gag?

DAPPER   Yes, faith, it crumbled
Away i' my mouth.

SUBTLE   You ha' spoil'd all then.

DAPPER   No!
I hope my aunt of Faery will forgive me.

SUBTLE   Your aunt's a gracious lady; but in troth
You were to blame.

DAPPER   The fume did overcome me,
And I did do't to stay my stomach. 'Pray you

So satisfy her Grace.

> [*Enter* FACE *in his uniform.*]

                    Here comes the Captain.
FACE   How now! Is his mouth down?
SUBTLE   Ay, he has spoken!
FACE [*Aside.*]   A pox, I heard him, and you too.
10   [*Aloud.*]   He's undone then.—
[*Aside to* SUBTLE.]   I have been fain to say, the house is haunted
With spirits, to keep churl back.
SUBTLE [*Aside.*]   And hast thou done it?
FACE [*Aside.*]   Sure, for this night.
SUBTLE [*Aside.*]   Why, then triumph and sing
Of Face so famous, the precious king
Of present wits.
FACE [*Aside.*]   Did you not hear the coil
About the door?
SUBTLE [*Aside.*]   Yes, and I dwindled with it.
20   FACE [*Aside.*]   Show him his aunt, and let him be dispatch'd:
I'll send her to you.   [*Exit* FACE.]
SUBTLE   Well, sir, your aunt her Grace
Will give you audience presently, on my suit,
And the Captain's word that you did not eat your gag
In any contempt of her Highness.   [*Unbinds his eyes.*]
DAPPER   Not I, in troth, sir.

> [*Enter*] DOL *like the Queen of Faery.*

SUBTLE   Here she is come. Down o' your knees and wriggle:
She has a stately presence. [DAPPER *kneels and shuffles toward
    her.*] Good! Yet nearer,
And bid, God save you!
DAPPER   Madam!
SUBTLE   And your aunt.
DAPPER   And my most gracious aunt, God save your Grace.
30   DOL COMMON   Nephew, we thought to have been angry
with you;
But that sweet face of yours hath turn'd the tide,
And made it flow with joy, that ebb'd of love.
Arise, and touch our velvet gown.
SUBTLE   The skirts,

17 **coil** disturbance

And kiss 'em. So!

DOL COMMON   Let me now stroke that head.
Much, nephew, shalt thou win, much shalt thou spend;
Much shalt thou give away; much shalt thou lend.

SUBTLE [*Aside.*]   Ay, much indeed!—Why do you not
thank her Grace?

DAPPER   I cannot speak for joy.

SUBTLE   See, the kind wretch!   40
Your Grace's kinsman right.

DOL COMMON   Give me the bird.—
Here is your fly in a purse, about your neck, cousin;
Wear it, and feed it about this day sev'n-night,
On your right wrist—

SUBTLE   Open a vein with a pin
And let it suck but once a week; till then,
You must not look on't.

DOL COMMON   No. And, kinsman,
Bear yourself worthy of the blood you come on.

SUBTLE   Her Grace would ha' you eat no more Woolsack
pies,
Nor Dagger frume'ty.

DOL COMMON   Nor break his fast   50
In Heaven and Hell.

SUBTLE   She's with you everywhere!
Nor play with costermongers, at mumchance, traytrip,
God-make-you-rich (when as your aunt has done it); but keep
The gallant'st company, and the best games—

DAPPER   Yes, sir.

SUBTLE   Gleek and primero; and what you get, be true
to us.

DAPPER   By this hand, I will.

SUBTLE   You may bring's a thousand pound
Before to-morrow night, if but three thousand
Be stirring, an you will.

DAPPER   I swear I will then.   60

SUBTLE   Your fly will learn you all games.

FACE [*Within.*]   Ha' you done there?

SUBTLE   Your Grace will command him no more duties?

DOL COMMON   No;
But come and see me often. I may chance

48 **Woolsack** a tavern 50 **frume'ty** wheat boiled in milk 51 **Heaven,
Hell** taverns 53 **mumchance . . . rich** games of chance 55 **Gleek, primero** card games

To leave him three or four hundred chests of treasure,
And some twelve thousand acres of fairy land,
If he game well and comely with good gamesters.
    SUBTLE   There's a kind aunt; kiss her departing part.—
But you must sell your forty mark a year now.
    DAPPER   Ay, sir, I mean.
    SUBTLE   Or, gi't away; pox on't!
70   DAPPER   I'll gi't mine aunt. I'll go and fetch the writings.
    SUBTLE   'Tis well; away.   [*Exit* DAPPER.]

               [*Re-enter* FACE.]

    FACE   Where's Subtle?
    SUBTLE   Here. What news?
    FACE   Drugger is at the door; go take his suit,
And bid him fetch a parson presently.
Say he shall marry the widow. Thou shalt spend
A hundred pound by the service!   [*Exit* SUBTLE.]
               Now, Queen Dol,
Have you pack'd up all?
    DOL COMMON   Yes.
    FACE   And how do you like
The Lady Pliant?
    DOL COMMON   A good dull innocent.

             [*Re-enter* SUBTLE.]

    SUBTLE   Here's your Hieronimo's cloak and hat.
    FACE   Give me 'em.
    SUBTLE   And the ruff too?
80   FACE   Yes; I'll come to you presently. [*Exit.*]
    SUBTLE   Now he is gone about his project, Dol,
I told you of, for the widow.
    DOL COMMON   'Tis direct
Against our articles.
    SUBTLE   Well, we'll fit him, wench.
Hast thou gull'd her of her jewels or her bracelets?
    DOL COMMON   No; but I will do't.
    SUBTLE   Soon at night, my Dolly,
When we are shipp'd and all our goods aboard,
Eastward for Ratcliff, we will turn our course
To Brainford, westward, if thou sayst the word,
And take our leaves of this o'erweening rascal,
This peremptory Face.
90   DOL COMMON   Content; I'm weary of him.

SUBTLE Thou'st cause, when the slave will run a-wiving, Dol,
Against the instrument that was drawn between us.
DOL COMMON I'll pluck his bird as bare as I can.
SUBTLE   Yes, tell her
She must by any means address some present
To th' cunning man, make him amends for wronging
His art with her suspicion; send a ring
Or chain of pearl; she will be tortur'd else
Extremely in her sleep, say, and ha' strange things
Come to her. Wilt thou?
DOL COMMON   Yes.
SUBTLE   My fine flitter-mouse,   100
My bird o' the night! We'll tickle it at the Pigeons,
When we have all, and may unlock the trunks,
And say, this's mine, and thine; and thine, and mine.
                                    They kiss.

[*Re-enter* FACE.]

FACE What now! a-billing?
SUBTLE   Yes, a little exalted
In the good passage of our stock-affairs.
FACE Drugger has brought his parson; take him in, Subtle,
And send Nab back again to wash his face.
SUBTLE I will. And shave himself?
FACE   If you can get him.
                                [*Exit* SUBTLE.]
DOL COMMON You are hot upon it, Face, whate'er it is!
FACE A trick that Dol shall spend ten pound a month by.   110

[*Re-enter* SUBTLE.]

Is he gone?
SUBTLE The chaplain waits you i' the hall, sir.
FACE I'll go bestow him.   [*Exit.*]
DOL COMMON   He'll now marry her instantly.
SUBTLE He cannot yet, he is not ready. Dear Dol,
Cozen her of all thou canst. To deceive him
Is no deceit, but justice, that would break
Such an inextricable tie as ours was.
DOL COMMON Let me alone to fit him.

[*Re-enter* FACE.]

FACE   Come, my venturers,

100 **flitter-mouse** bat 101 **Pigeons** an inn at Brainford

You ha' pack'd up all? Where be the trunks? Bring forth.

120 SUBTLE Here.

FACE Let's see 'em. Where's the money?

SUBTLE Here,
In this.

FACE Mammon's ten pound; eight score before.
The Brethren's money this. Drugger's and Dapper's?
What paper's that?

DOL COMMON The jewel of the waiting maid's,
That stole it from her lady, to know certain—

FACE If she should have precedence of her mistress?

DOL COMMON Yes.

FACE What box is that?

SUBTLE The fish-wives' rings, I think,
130 And th'ale-wives' single money. Is't not, Dol?

DOL COMMON Yes, and the whistle that the sailor's wife
Brought you to know an her husband were with Ward.

FACE We'll wet it to-morrow; and our silver beakers
And tavern cups. Where be the French petticoats
And girdles and hangers?

SUBTLE Here, i' the trunk,
And the bolts of lawn.

FACE Is Drugger's damask there,
And the tobacco?

SUBTLE Yes.

FACE Give me the keys.

DOL COMMON Why you the keys?

SUBTLE No matter, Dol; because
We shall not open 'em before he comes.

140 FACE 'Tis true, you shall not open them, indeed;
Nor have 'em forth, do you see? Not forth, Dol.

DOL COMMON No!

FACE No, my smock-rampant. The right is, my master
Knows all, has pardon'd me, and he will keep 'em.
Doctor, 'tis true—you look—for all your figures!
I sent for him, indeed. Wherefore, good partners,
Both he and she, be satisfied; for here
Determines the indenture tripartite
'Twixt Subtle, Dol, and Face. All I can do
150 Is to help you over the wall, o' the back-side,
Or lend you a sheet to save your velvet gown, Dol.

130 **single-money** small change 132 **Ward** a famous pirate 143 **right**
fact 148 **Determines** terminates

Here will be officers presently; bethink you
Of some course suddenly to scape the dock;
For thither you'll come else. [*Violent knocking at the door.*]
        Hark you, thunder.

SUBTLE You are a precious fiend!

OFFICERS [*Without.*]   Open the door.

FACE Dol, I am sorry for thee, i' faith; but hear'st thou?
It shall go hard but I will place thee somewhere.
Thou shalt ha' my letter to Mistress Amo—

DOL COMMON   Hang you!

FACE Or Madam Cæsarean.

DOL COMMON   Pox upon you, rogue,   160
Would I had but time to beat thee!

FACE   Subtle,
Let's know where you set up next; I'll send you
A customer now and then, for old acquaintance.
What new course ha' you?

SUBTLE   Rogue, I'll hang myself,
That I may walk a greater devil than thou,
And haunt thee i' the flock-bed and the buttery.

               [*Exeunt.*]

Scene V

[*Enter* LOVEWIT *in a Spanish costume, with the Parson.
Knocking at the door continues.*]

[LOVEWIT] What do you mean, my masters?

MAMMON [*Without.*]   Open your door,
Cheaters, bawds, conjurers.

OFFICER [*Without.*] Or we'll break it open.

LOVEWIT What warrant have you?

OFFICER [*Without.*]   Warrant enough, sir, doubt not,
If you'll not open it.

LOVEWIT   Is there an officer there?

OFFICER [*Without.*] Yes, two or three for failing.

LOVEWIT   Have but patience,
And I will open it straight.

   [*Enter* FACE *in his butler's livery.*]

FACE   Sir, ha' you done?

159 **Mistress Amo, Madam Cæsarean** mistresses of brothels 166 **flock-
bed . . . buttery** at bed and board

Is it a marriage? Perfect?

LOVEWIT   Yes, my brain.

FACE   Off with your ruff and cloak then; be yourself, sir.

SURLY [*Without.*]   Down with the door.

KASTRIL [*Without.*]   'Slight, ding it open.

LOVEWIT [*Opening the door.*]   Hold,
10 Hold, gentlemen, what means this violence?

[MAMMON, SURLY, KASTRIL, ANANIAS, TRIBULATION, *and*
OFFICERS *rush in.*]

MAMMON   Where is this collier?

SURLY   And my Captain Face?

MAMMON   These day-owls.

SURLY   That are birding in men's purses.

MAMMON   Madam Suppository.

KASTRIL   Doxy, my suster.

ANANIAS   Locusts
Of the foul pit.

TRIBULATION   Profane as Bel and the Dragon.

ANANIAS   Worse than the grasshoppers, or the lice of Egypt.

LOVEWIT   Good gentlemen, hear me. Are you officers,
And cannot stay this violence?

OFFICER   Keep the peace.

LOVEWIT   Gentlemen, what is the matter? Whom do you
20 seek?

MAMMON   The chemical cozener.

SURLY   And the captain pandar.

KASTRIL   The nun my suster.

MAMMON   Madam Rabbi.

ANANIAS   Scorpions,
And caterpillars.

LOVEWIT   Fewer at once, I pray you.

OFFICER   One after another, gentlemen, I charge you,
By virtue of my staff.

ANANIAS   They are the vessels
Of pride, lust, and the cart.

LOVEWIT   Good zeal, lie still
A little while.

TRIBULATION   Peace, Deacon Ananias.

LOVEWIT   The house is mine here, and the doors are open;
If there be any such persons as you seek for,
30 Use your authority, search on o' God's name.
I am but newly come to town, and finding

12 **birding** pilfering

This tumult 'bout my door, to tell you true,
It somewhat maz'd me; till my man here, fearing
My more displeasure, told me he had done
Somewhat an insolent part, let out my house
(Belike presuming on my known aversion
From any air o' the town while there was sickness),
To a doctor and a captain; who, what they are
Or where they be, he knows not.

MAMMON   Are they gone?
LOVEWIT You may go in and search, sir.   *They enter*.
                          Here, I find   40
The empty walls worse than I left 'em, smok'd,
A few crack'd pots, and glasses, and a furnace;
The ceiling fill'd with poesies of the candle,
And "Madam with a dildo" writ o' the walls.
Only one gentlewoman I met here,
That is within, that said she was a widow—

KASTRIL Ay, that's my suster; I'll go thump her. Where
    is she?   [*Goes in*.]
LOVE And should ha' married a Spanish count, but he,
When he came to 't, neglected her so grossly,
That I, a widower, am gone through with her.   50
SURLY How! have I lost her, then?
LOVEWIT   Were you the don, sir?
Good faith, now, she does blame you extremely, and says
You swore, and told her you had ta'en the pains
To dye your beard, and umber o'er your face,
Borrow'd a suit and ruff, all for her love:
And then did nothing. What an oversight
And want of putting forward, sir, was this!
Well fare an old harquebusier yet,
Could prime his powder, and give fire, and hit,
All in a twinkling!   MAMMON *comes forth*.
MAMMON   The whole nest are fled!   60
LOVEWIT What sort of birds were they?
MAMMON   A kind of choughs,
Or thievish daws, sir, that have pick'd my purse
Of eight score and ten pounds within these five weeks,
Beside my first materials; and my goods,
That lie i' the cellar, which I am glad they ha' left,
I may have home yet.

44 **Madam . . . dildo** refrain of popular ballad   58 **harquebusier**
musketeer

LOVEWIT   Think you so, sir?
MAMMON   Ay.
LOVEWIT   By order of law, sir, but not otherwise.
MAMMON   Not mine own stuff?
LOVEWIT   Sir, I can take no knowledge
That they are yours, but by public means.
70 If you can bring certificate that you were gull'd of 'em,
Or any formal writ out of a court,
That you did cozen yourself, I will not hold them.
      MAMMON   I'll rather lose 'em.
      LOVEWIT   That you shall not, sir,
By me, in troth. Upon these terms, they're yours.
What, should they ha' been, sir, turn'd into gold, all?
      MAMMON   No.
I cannot tell.—It may be they should.—What then?
      LOVEWIT   What a great loss in hope have you sustain'd!
      MAMMON   Not I; the commonwealth has.
      FACE   Ay, he would ha' built
80 The city new; and made a ditch about it
Of silver, should have run with cream from Hogsden;
That every Sunday in Moorfields the younkers
And tits and tom-boys should have fed on, gratis.
      MAMMON   I will go mount a turnip-cart, and preach
The end o' the world within these two months.—Surly,
What! in a dream?
      SURLY   Must I needs cheat myself
With that same foolish vice of honesty!
Come, let us go and hearken out the rogues.
That Face I'll mark for mine, if e'er I meet him.
90   FACE   If I can hear of him, sir, I'll bring you word
Unto your lodging; for in troth, they were strangers
To me; I thought 'em honest as myself, sir.
                          [*Exeunt* SURLY *and* MAMMON.]

            [*Re-enter* ANANIAS *and* TRIBULATION.]

TRIBULATION   'Tis well, the saints shall not lose all yet. Go
And get some carts—
      LOVEWIT   For what, my zealous friends?
      ANANIAS   To bear away the portion of the righteous
Out of this den of thieves.
      LOVEWIT   What is that portion?

82 **younkers** young men 83 **tits** wenches 88 **hearken** search

ANANIAS   The goods, sometimes the orphans', that the
Brethren bought with their silver pence.

LOVEWIT   What, those i' the cellar,
The knight Sir Mammon claims?

ANANIAS   I do defy
The wicked Mammon, so do all the Brethren.   100
Thou profane man! I ask thee with what conscience
Thou canst advance that idol against us
That have the seal? Were not the shillings numb'red
That made the pounds; were not the pounds told out
Upon the second day of the fourth week,
In the eight month, upon the table dormant,
The year of the last patience of the saints,
Six hundred and ten?

LOVEWIT   Mine earnest vehement botcher,
And deacon also, I cannot dispute with you;   110
But if you get you not away the sooner,
I shall confute you with a cudgel.

ANANIAS   Sir!

TRIBULATION   Be patient, Ananias.

ANANIAS   I am strong,
And will stand up, well girt, against an host
That threaten Gad in exile.

LOVEWIT   I shall send you
To Amsterdam, to your cellar.

ANANIAS   I will pray there,
Against thy house. May dogs defile thy walls,
And wasps and hornets breed beneath thy roof,
This seat of falsehood, and this cave of coz'nage!

[*Exeunt* ANANIAS *and* TRIBULATION.]

DRUGGER *enters.*

LOVEWIT   Another too?

DRUGGER   Not I, sir, I am no Brother.   120

LOVEWIT   Away, you Harry Nicholas! do you talk?

                              He beats him away.

FACE   No, this was Abel Drugger. (*To the Parson.*) Good
sir, go,
And satisfy him; tell him all is done.

97 **sometimes** formerly 103 **have the seal** are sealed as God's people
121 **Harry Nicholas** a notorious religious fanatic 122 **Parson** *i.e.,* the
local parson who came in with Lovewit, but who has said nothing.

He stay'd too long a-washing of his face.
The Doctor, he shall hear of him at Westchester;
And of the Captain, tell him, at Yarmouth, or
Some good port-town else, lying for a wind.

[*Exit* PARSON.]

If you get off the angry child now, sir—

[*Enter* KASTRIL, *dragging in his sister* DAME PLIANT.]

KASTRIL   Come on, you ewe, you have match'd most
130   sweetly, ha' you not?
Did not I say, I would never ha' you tupp'd
But by a dubb'd boy, to make you a lady-tom?
'Slight, you are a mammet! O, I could touse you now.
Death, mun you marry with a pox!
LOVEWIT   You lie, boy;
As sound as you; and I'm aforehand with you.
KASTRIL   Anon?
LOVEWIT   Come, will you quarrel? I will feize you, sirrah;
Why do you not buckle to your tools?
KASTRIL   God's light,
This is a fine old boy as e'er I saw!
LOVEWIT   What, do you change your copy now? Proceed;
140   Here stands my dove: stoop at her if you dare.
KASTRIL   'Slight, I must love him! I cannot choose, i' faith,
An I should be hang'd for't! Suster, I protest,
I honour thee for this match.
LOVEWIT   O, do you so, sir?
KASTRIL   Yes, an thou canst take tobacco and drink, old
boy,
I'll give her five hundred pound more to her marriage,
Than her own state.
LOVEWIT   Fill a pipe full, Jeremy.
FACE   Yes; but go in and take it, sir.
LOVEWIT   We will.
I will be rul'd by thee in anything, Jeremy.
150   KASTRIL   'Slight, thou art not hide-bound, thou art a jovy
boy!
Come, let's in, I pray thee, and take our whiffs.
LOVEWIT   Whiff in with your sister, brother boy.

[*Exeunt* KASTRIL *and* DAME PLIANT.]

132 **dubb'd boy** knight 133 **mammet** puppet **touse** handle roughly
134 **mun** must 135 **Anon** Eh? 136 **feize** beat 140 **stoop** swoop (a term
in falconry) 150 **jovy** jovial

That master

That had receiv'd such happiness by a servant,
In such a widow, and with so much wealth,
Were very ungrateful, if he would not be
A little indulgent to that servant's wit,
And help his fortune, though with some small strain
Of his own candour.   [*Advancing for the epilogue and
addressing the audience.*]
        Therefore, gentlemen,
And kind spectators, if I have outstripp'd   160
An old man's gravity, or strict canon, think
What a young wife and a good brain may do:
Stretch age's truth sometimes, and crack it too.
Speak for thyself, knave.

    FACE   So I will, sir. [*Advancing to the front of the stage.*]
        Gentlemen,
My part a little fell in this last scene,
Yet 'twas decorum. And though I am clean
Got off from Subtle, Surly, Mammon, Dol,
Hot Ananias, Dapper, Drugger, all
With whom I traded; yet I put myself   170
On you, that are my country; and this pelf
Which I have got, if you do quit me, rests,
To feast you often, and invite new guests.

                                        [*Exeunt.*]

---

159 **candour** integrity 167 **decorum** dramatic propriety 171 **country**
jury (legal term) 172 **quit** acquit

Bibliography

I

Herford, C. H. and Percy and Evelyn Simpson, *Ben Jonson,* 11 volumes, Oxford, 1925-53.

Levin, Harry, *Ben Jonson: Selected Works,* New York, 1938.

Newdigate, Bernard H., *The Poems of Ben Jonson,* Oxford, 1936.

II

Barish, Jonas A., *Ben Jonson: A Collection of Critical Essays,* Englewood Cliffs, New Jersey, 1963.

Chute, Marchette, *Ben Jonson of Westminster,* New York, 1953.

Enck, John J., *Ben Jonson and the Comic Truth,* Madison, Wisconsin, 1957.

Linklater, Eric, *Ben Jonson and King James: A Biography and a Portrait,* London, 1931.

Redwine, James, "Beyond Psychology: The Moral Basis of Jonson's Theory of Humour Characterization," *English Literary History* XXVIII (December, 1961) 316-334.

III

Bentley, Gerald Eades, *The Jacobean and Caroline Stage,* Vols. I-V, Oxford, 1941- (in progress).

Chambers, E. K., *The Elizabethan Stage,* 4 volumes. Oxford, 1923.

Harrison, G. B., *A Jacobean Journal; being a record of those things most talked of during the years 1603-1606,* London, 1941.

———— *A Second Jacobean Journal; being a record of those things most talked of during the years 1607-1610,* Ann Arbor, Michigan, 1958.

Knights, L. C., *Drama and Society in the Age of Jonson,* London, 1937.

Nicoll, Allardyce, *Stuart Masques and the Renaissance Stage,* New York, 1938.